GOES TO THE

GROUND

LORI O'CONNELL

Foreword by **Steve Hiscoe** and **Jennifer Weintz**

TUTTLE Publishing

Tokyo | Rutland, Vermont | Singapore

Please note that the publisher and author(s) of this instructional book are NOT RESPONSIBLE in any manner whatsoever for any injury that may result from practicing the techniques and/or following the instructions given within. Martial arts training can be dangerous—both to you and to others—if not practiced safely. If you're in doubt as to how to proceed or whether your practice is safe, consult with a trained martial arts teacher before beginning. Since the physical activities described herein may be too strenuous in nature for some readers, it is also essential that a physician be consulted prior to training.

Published by Tuttle Publishing, an imprint of Periplus Editions (HK) Ltd.

www.tuttlepublishing.com

Copyright © 2012 Lori O'Connell

Library of Congress Cataloging-in-Publication Data
In Process

ISBN 978-0-8048-4253-2

Distributed by

North America, Latin America & Europe	Japan	Asia Pacific
Tuttle Publishing	Tuttle Publishing	Berkeley Books Pte. Ltd.
364 Innovation Drive	Yaekari Building,	61 Tai Seng Avenue
North Clarendon, VT	3rd Floor, 5-4-12 Osaki	#02-12,
05759-9436 U.S.A.	Shinagawa-ku	Singapore 534167
Tel: 1 (802) 773-8930	Tokyo 141 0032	Tel: (65) 6280-1330
Fax: 1 (802) 773-6993	Tel: (81) 3 5437-0171	Fax: (65) 6280-6290
info@tuttlepublishing.com	Fax: (81) 3 5437-0755	inquiries@periplus.com.sg
www.tuttlepublishing.com	sales@tuttle.co.jp	www.periplus.com
	www.tuttle.co.jp	

First edition
15 14 13 12   5 4 3 2 1   1110RP

Printed in Singapore

TUTTLE PUBLISHING® is a registered trademark of Tuttle Publishing, a division of Periplus Editions (HK) Ltd.

Contents

The Tuttle Story: "Books to Span the East and West"

Most people are surprised to learn that the world's largest publisher of books on Asia had its humble beginnings in the tiny American state of Vermont. The company's founder, Charles Tuttle, came from a New England family steeped in publishing, and his first love was books—especially old and rare editions.

Tuttle's father was a noted antiquarian dealer in Rutland, Vermont. Young Charles honed his knowledge of the trade working in the family bookstore, and later in the rare books section of Columbia University Library. His passion for beautiful books—old and new—never wavered throughout his long career as a bookseller and publisher.

After graduating from Harvard, Tuttle enlisted in the military and in 1945 was sent to Tokyo to work on General Douglas MacArthur's staff. He was tasked with helping to revive the Japanese publishing industry, which had been utterly devastated by the war. When his tour of duty was completed, he left the military, married a talented and beautiful singer, Reiko Chiba, and in 1948 began several successful business ventures.

To his astonishment, Tuttle discovered that postwar Tokyo was actually a book-lover's paradise. He befriended dealers in the Kanda district and began supplying rare Japanese editions to American libraries. He also imported American books to sell to the thousands of GIs stationed in Japan. By 1949, Tuttle's business was thriving, and he opened Tokyo's very first English-language bookstore in the Takashimaya Department Store in Ginza, to great success. Two years later, he began publishing books to fulfill the growing interest of foreigners in all things Asian.

Though a westerner, Tuttle was hugely instrumental in bringing a knowledge of Japan and Asia to a world hungry for information about the East. By the time of his death in 1993, he had published over 6,000 books on Asian culture, history and art—a legacy honored by Emperor Hirohito in 1983 with the "Order of the Sacred Treasure," the highest honor Japan bestows upon non-Japanese.

The Tuttle company today maintains an active backlist of some 1,500 titles, many of which have been continuously in print since the 1950s and 1960s—a great testament to Charles Tuttle's skill as a publisher. More than 60 years after its founding, Tuttle Publishing is more active today than at any time in its history, still inspired by Charles Tuttle's core mission—to publish fine books to span the East and West and provide a greater understanding of each.

Acknowledgments

This book is the culmination of many people's efforts and support for which I am extremely grateful. These simple "acknowledgments" just don't do enough to fully express my thanks, but it's a start.

A huge thank you to Chris Olson, my right hand man who dutifully allowed me to work through all my concepts as I wrote, only to have to do it all again for the camera then spend hours upon hours picking out the shots that best conveyed the action (as well as his own pain).

Ed Hiscoe Hanshi, my Sensei, deserves thanks, but so much more. I always look to his example for his passion for teaching self-defense but also helping people grow. He stood behind me throughout all my early training years, even those difficult upstart years while I moved from the impetuousness of adolescence into the reckoning of adulthood.

Steve Hiscoe Shihan picked up where he left off after I moved to British Columbia. He has continued to guide me in my development with the soft hand of a benevolent leader. I am thankful for all his advice and support, as well as his continued commitment to uniting all the practitioners of our style.

Professor Georges Sylvain, founder of Can-ryu, deserves the utmost gratitude, from me and all the students who have felt his influence directly or indirectly, for his decades of devotion to the development of our style. It was Professor Sylvain who once took me aside after a black belt training session to tell me my potential as a martial artist, a conversation which touched me deeply and has continued to motivate me to be the best I can be.

Thank you to Glenn Chow (glennjitsu@gmail.com) for being the eye behind the camera and spending many hours getting the right shots to convey my vision. Thank you also to his family for giving him up during all those valuable weekend hours.

Kevin MacDonald is truly deserving of a shout-out as one of the attackers, having instructed me to apply some of the more painful techniques with gusto to get the right reactions from him since he is, in his words, "not much of an actor."

Thank you to Jennifer Weintz who in a few short training sessions, taught me a number of concepts that helped me even the odds against much bigger grappling opponents, which served to refine my approach to ground defense. Her example is an inspiration to martial artists everywhere, male or female.

I also want to thank all the other instructors who have taught me over the years and inspired me to continually progress, with special mentions going out to Robert Mustard Sensei, Andy Dobie Sensei, Michael Seamark Shihan, and Perry William Kelly Sensei.

Thanks to all my training buddies who made themselves available to help me work on my book by asking questions, putting pressure on my concepts, and play testing them, including Jonathan Jamnik, Stu Cooke, Jon Thompson and Matt Der.

My students have also been a rock of support through the writing of my book, cheerleading me on as I finished each chapter, reminding me who it's all for.

A big thank you also goes out to Bud Sperry, who "found" me, believed in my vision, and supported my book from proposal, to editing, and all the way through to publication.

Last, but not least, I want to thank my parents who raised me to be driven, strong-willed and compassionate. I may not have followed the path of a "traditional" woman, and they may not understand all that I do, but they have always stood behind me and been excited to share in my joys and successes.

Foreword by Steve Hiscoe

Photo by Leann Parker.

Daily law enforcement officers are called in to intervene and manage situations that the general public are unable to solve. These situations can range from trivial in nature to affecting the arrest of violent individuals. These arrests can sometimes lead to physical confrontations resulting in all-out-knock-down-drag-'em-out fights. That being said, it is inevitable that officers will find themselves, at some point in their career, fighting on the ground. Over the past 20 years, the law enforcement community has seen the introduction of new and innovative intervention options, such as pepper spray, defensive batons, and conducted energy weapons (tasers) added to their duty belts. Moreover, the physical description of police officers has changed dramatically, from mostly physically large males, to a diverse workforce, which includes men and women of all shapes, sizes, and ages.

As such police training has seen the emphasis move away from physical hands on combative style training to more of a reliance on the use of intermediate intervention options. The result is that during any arrest situations police officers bring weapons with them. Therefore during a ground fight, these weapons are difficult to access for the officer and could also be available for the subject to grab. Therefore, when you're rolling around in the mud, the blood and the beer, the goal is not to submit but rather to control your suspect and get them handcuffed. Bad guys are learning to ground fight from watching television and would take extreme pleasure from making a cop "tap out." Unfortunately, tapping out is not an option for a cop.

As a martial artist of 35 years and 20+ year veteran police officer, I have found myself in many arrest situations where a suspect has wanted to hurt me or take me to the ground. My ability to recognize pre-attack threat cues and take action immediately has kept me safe. As a police officer the last place I want to be is on the ground. I am also a national level Public and Police Safety Instructor with the Royal Canadian Mounted Police (R.C.M.P). As such, I have had the opportunity to participate and evaluate several ground fighting programs advertised as being for law enforcement. Many of these programs have simply taken the sport application and attempted to apply it to law enforcement, which is not that easy.

I first met Lori O'Connell Sensei about 10 years ago when she moved to the Vancouver area of British Columbia, Canada. After meeting at several training seminars and camps that I had hosted, it was not difficult to recognize her enthusiasm and passion for jiu-jitsu and the martial arts. During these past 10 years she has become the highest ranking woman in Can-Ryu in all of Western Canada. To challenge herself and take her learning to the next level, she began to explore BJJ and MMA concepts related to ground fighting. Lori was also seeking how to incorporate this knowledge into the Can-Ryu system. Recognizing her talent and extreme energy for the topic, I personally asked her to review our curriculum's existing ground defense techniques and see where improvements could be made. I did place one condition on her research; that the techniques had to be consistent with the existing principles of our style. Lori accepted the challenge and put her analytical to mind to work. Lori spent many hours trying out new techniques and counter tactics while taking her own physical attributes into consideration. You see, Lori is about 5'3" and weighs around 124 pounds, which means she cannot rely on her size to control someone, she has to rely on her technique.

Lori conducted a seminar to demonstrate the techniques to our black belt instructors, the techniques were so well received that I decided to include them in our main curriculum.

In my professional opinion, I believe the information you will find in this book to be extremely valuable to your safety and personal well-being. Any instructor who teaches self-defense should have this book in their resource library.

—Steven Hiscoe Shihan
8th Degree Black Belt Can-Ryu Jiu-Jitsu
Owner/Chief Instructor Hiscoe Jiu-Jitsu
Vice –President Canadian Jiu-Jitsu Union
Chilliwack, British Columbia

Foreword by Jennifer Weintz

Photo by Michael Palmer.

Having trained in Brazilian Jiu-jitsu (BJJ) for over 10 years, I've developed a long-standing love affair with the cerebral nature of the art. I love the ebb and flow of two energies merging as the roles of attacker and defender shift back and forth in an extended physical chess match. The artistry of the style is something I've come to appreciate over the years the more I've tuned in to its subtleties through many countless hours of developing my craft.

The focus of my grappling training has been primarily competition oriented, but I am fully aware that these same ground fighting techniques are also useful in real-life self-defense scenarios. As a smaller woman, I've learned how to "take the path of least resistance" and use speed, agility and finesse to hold my own. That being said, there are important factors to defending one's self on the street that aren't present in the competitive arena. This naturally raises questions like: What if my attacker tried to kick me in head? What if my attacker pulled a knife? What if there was more than one attacker? What if my attacker is so much bigger and stronger than me that finesse isn't enough?

Lori O'Connell answers these questions and many more in this book, addressing issues that are not always regularly discussed in submission grappling schools. It provides a complete look at all the major positions and defensive situations, with detailed, easy-to-follow instruction that walks you through every move step-by-step, making it an ideal choice for learning practical, effective techniques for real-life self-protection.

Over the course of my training, I've discovered the importance of keeping an open mind and learning from people of all walks of life to refine and add to my set of skills. Both men and women, beginners and experts, people with training in BJJ and even other martial art styles can have something to offer. An opportunity to learn can always be found. Being a smaller woman herself,

Lori knows what it's like to be at a physical disadvantage and understands what it takes to overcome it to escape dangerous situations, ones you may not necessarily be able to "tap" your way out of. So if you're looking to learn to make the most of a bad situation, fighting from the ground without rules or refs to keep you safe, and the odds stacked against you, you've come to the right place.

—Jennifer Weintz
Brazilian Jiu-jitsu Brown Belt
2-time Pan-American Champion

Introduction

On November 12, 1993, the UFC made its debut with the Gracie family introducing their style of Brazilian Jiu-jitsu (BJJ) to the world. This event changed the martial arts world forever. Prior to that time, the vast majority of martial arts schools focused solely on stand-up styles, with little, if any, coverage on what to do if a fight goes to the ground. While the UFC started in 1993, it took a few years before it started to become more mainstream, but by the end of the 90s, BJJ schools started popping up all over North America, and throughout the world.

The publicity the Gracie family received for their style was massive. Suddenly, everyone wanted to learn this "new" art that had stepped up against representatives of a variety of styles in a "no rules" competitive format, beating them out one by one. The average Joe saw BJJ as the new "ultimate" fighting system. People flocked to BJJ schools in droves.

As the years went by, the nature of the UFC changed. Competitors came to realize the deficiencies of training in a single martial arts style. Competitors learned that they needed to train in multiple styles and have a mix of skills including stand-up striking, throws/takedowns, and ground fighting, in order to compete effectively in UFC fights. It no longer pitted one style against another. It evolved to create a new breed of martial art, simply called Mixed Martial Arts or "MMA." The Gracie family no longer dominated the UFC ring, but BJJ would always have a place in MMA as the ground grappling aspect, which people came to commonly refer to as "Jiu-jitsu."

Origins of Can-ryu Jiu-jitsu

The year the UFC began was the same year I started my martial arts career. At that time, I was completely unaware of the existence of UFC and Brazilian jiu-jitsu. The only jiu-jitsu I had ever heard of was Japanese jiu-jitsu, and the style I signed up to learn was one such variant, known as Can-ryu Jiu-jitsu or "Canadian Style of Jiu-jitsu." This style combined stand-up striking, throws/takedowns, joint locks, ground combat and weapon defense. It was a "mixed" martial art before the term came to carry different connotations, created by Professor Georges Sylvain, a "mixed martial artist" in his own right.

Now retired, Professor Sylvain holds a 10th degree black belt in jiu-jitsu, 4th degree black belt in karate, and has also trained extensively in Western boxing and judo. A Black Belt Hall of Fame inductee, he has also been acclaimed by the martial arts community for his pioneering work in developing and innovating training methods for the sport of kickboxing. In addition to his martial arts training background, Professor Sylvain served as a Canadian Military Police officer during the Korean War and as an Ottawa Municipal Police officer for 15 years. He is also a Tactical Training Officer with an international reputation. He was the Chief Instructor of physical defense training at Algonquin College in Ottawa for its Law and Security program, having taught there for 25 years, in addition to having been Chief Instructor to RCMP self-defense instructors in Rockliffe, Ontario before they were relocated to Western Canada. He was also the first Canadian police trainer ever to have been invited as a guest lecturer at the Smith-Wesson Police Academy in 1989. In addition to his instructive capacities, Professor Sylvain has served as an expert witness in self-defense and has testified on the behalf of a number of police officers.

For many years, Professor Sylvain had focused his attention solely in the area of law enforcement, having removed himself from the formal business of the martial arts world entirely. But one day he decided to reclaim his place in the style he created, in conjunction with my Sensei, Ed Hiscoe Hanshi (currently 9th degree black belt). In doing so, he reaffirmed an emphasis on the original spirit of his style through the base tenets of Can-ryu Jiu-jitsu, which he felt had fallen away. Since Professor Sylvain's retirement, my Sensei has been appointed the new head of style with his son, Steve Hiscoe Shihan (8th degree black belt) named as the heir apparent. Steve Hiscoe Shihan is also a 20-year veteran RCMP member with the rank of Corporal, currently assigned to the RCMP Training Academy in Chilliwack and is responsible for training and coordinating the assignments of the academy's instructors.

The Modernization of Can-Ryu Ground Defense

As I started to teach Can-ryu Jiu-jitsu, I became more aware of the UFC and BJJ as its impact on the martial arts world grew over time. More and more new students showing up to try classes at our dojo came to us mistakenly looking for a place to learn BJJ. We learned that we had to more clearly distinguish how we were different from the Brazilian off-shoot, focusing more on self-protection rather than competition. More than that, we learned that we also needed to update our ground defense skills to address its changing nature, as well as the greater variety of moves that had become more commonplace due to the popularity of UFC and BJJ. It wasn't just that more people were officially learning ground fighting skills at martial arts schools. A great number were also learning simply by watching UFC fights, as well as YouTube videos that were widely available on the Internet.

Prior to the influence of the UFC and BJJ and before Professor Sylvain re-engaged himself in the martial arts community, our ground defense system comprised of a set of defenses against what were considered common holds and attacks on the ground. The problem with that method of training was that it was overly prescribed and didn't address the dynamic nature of ground fighting. Some of the defenses also relied on techniques that kept the defender prone on the ground, leaving them open to attacks from additional attackers.

Professor Sylvain brought us back to the focus of getting to our feet as quickly as possible. The first line of defense he taught when you were on the ground and your attacker was on his feet was to keep your legs between you and your attacker, kicking at vulnerable targets as they tried to move in. We were taught to control their legs and take them down if possible. There was little emphasis on what to do if the attacker managed to get on top of you. He said simply that we should "launch an all-out attack against the most accessible, vulnerable areas of his body." The idea was that we were to try to get an immediate advantage create an opportunity to get off the ground as quickly as possible. This is a very important foundation often completely ignored in modern ground fighting systems designed more for competitive purposes. It did, however, leave much open to interpretation as to how best to apply this principle.

To try and fill this void, I started doing some side training in BJJ and MMA, to learn new defensive tactics to combine with my Can-ryu skills. Over time, I developed a modernized, simplified approach to ground defense to cover the gap left by Professor Sylvain's very open concept, one that was practical and adaptable for different body types that more closely fit with the self-protection tenets of our style. Having seen some of these defense methods, I was eventually asked by Steve Hiscoe Shihan several years ago to provide the foundation for an updated ground defense curriculum for our style.

Lori O'Connell doing MMA training

Before you ask, no I do not have a black belt in BJJ, nor a competitive record in MMA. My goal in training in these arts was never to achieve ranks, but to learn what I needed to equip my students for self-protection against the realities of modern ground fighting. I've trained in jiu-jitsu for over 20 years and hold the rank of 4th degree in my style. Being a small woman, I've had to develop a set of defensive skills and tactics that make up for my disadvantages in size and strength. The ground defense system I've put together is designed with a "worst case scenario" mindset that is meant to be usable even if the attacker has a major size and strength advantage as most attacks don't come from people who are smaller and weaker than you. That being said, I've also included variations in this book to address scenarios in which different body types affect the way a person can move.

Who Can Use This Book

I wrote this book with three types of martial artists in mind. Most BJJ and MMA schools teach their arts specifically for the competitive arena. If you're a student in this type of school with a desire to learn to apply your skills for self-protection in a street-oriented assault situation, this book will teach you concepts and techniques you can combine with your training for application in this context. There are also many traditional martial arts schools that focus on a single stand-up striking style with little to no defensive techniques for the ground. If you're a student at such a school and would like to learn a simple, effective system of ground combat you can combine with your stand-up defensive skills, this book has you covered. The last type of martial artist is the one most likely to actually use these skills, but oftentimes spends the least amount of time training. Because of the temporary nature of the physical defense training programs and their demanding schedules, many police officers have very little experience training ground defense skills. This simple ground defense system provides skills they can learn quickly and easily apply on the job.

The ground defense system in this book is NOT a complete system of self-protection. It covers only one aspect to be partnered with other strategies and defensive techniques, including soft skills like personal awareness, conflict avoidance, and de-escalation tactics, as well as hard/physical skills, such as stand-up striking, throws, and takedowns, etc. Nevertheless, ground defense is an important skill to learn if one's goal is to have a well-rounded system of self-protection.

How to Use this Book

This book teaches self-protection from the ground in a variety of ways. It provides information and concepts that help you understand the realities of fighting from the ground, as well as information on the defensive advantages and disadvantages that are inherent in different combat situations. It teaches you the basic tools of physical defense on the ground, body shifting/positional strategy and attacks to vital targets, which combine to give you a foundation that can be adapted for different situations, body types, situational factors, etc. It also provides detailed descriptions with photos showing you a number of examples of how the basic tools can be used to mount an effective defense. These examples help you consider different ways of applying your skills, but don't let them bind you. Real physical combat is an entity in itself. Everything can change in an instant. Attackers don't necessarily react the way you expect. You have to be adaptive and ready for anything. Your attacker could be so high or drunk that they don't react to pain. Or your first strike could knock them out or simply dissuade them from pursuing further aggressive action. You may even find yourself reacting in a way that you never trained but made sense at the time. Keep an open mind, whether you're training your defensive skills or your reacting to a real live attacker. As leaders in my style have said countless times in the past: Never say always. Never say never. There are no rules, only results.

CHAPTER 1

Understanding the Ground

It is important to recognize the nature of ground defense in a street context to be able to fully understand the logic behind the techniques featured in this book. More than that, knowing the nature of ground defense helps anyone interested in self-protection to realize its place in an overall defensive strategy.

Statistics on Ground Fighting

If you have any interest in the martial arts or self-defense, you have probably heard the often quoted "statistic" that 80-90 percent of physical altercations end up on the ground. I, myself, heard this statistic quoted often enough throughout the entirety of my 20+ year career in the martial arts. Not once did I ever hear the source of said statistic. It was simply "common knowledge" that everyone accepted as fact.

There are two legitimate sources that I am aware of that have presented statistics on this topic. One of them is the ASLET (American Society of Law Enforcement Training) pamphlet used from their July 1997 Use of Force Training Seminar. The seminar was presented in Los Angeles by Sergeant Greg Dossey, Sergeant John Sommers, and Officer Steve Uhrig of the Los Angeles Police Department (LAPD). This document included a description of the study and methodology used in examining Use of Force incidents by the LAPD. In 1991, Sergeant Dossey completed a comparative study of use of force incidents reported by the LAPD for the year of 1988. He looked at all 5,617 use of force incident narratives written by officers for that year, and devised a method for codifying the information contained and analyzing it for what they identified as dominant altercation patterns. The study was replicated in 1992 by the LAPD's Training Review committee.

One of the main conclusions of the report was that "Nearly two thirds of the 1988 altercations (62%) ended with the officer and subject on the ground with the officer applying a joint lock and handcuffing the subject." After this report was published, the LAPD instituted a program that included training in ground control skills, which were based on modern judo and jiu-jitsu grappling skills specially adapted for law enforcement.

The other source of credible ground fighting statistics comes from Calibre Press's April 2003 newsletter. They published the results of a research project completed in conjunction with PPCT Management Systems. This project measured the frequency in which police officers were forced to the ground by attackers, based on 1,400 cases reported by officers attending Calibre Press's annual Street Survival Seminar.[*]

Respondents were asked whether an attacker had ever attempted to take them to the ground by force. Fifty percent reported this had occurred to them. Of that number, 60% reported that their attackers had been successful in doing so. Most of the attackers were reported as having been under the influence of alcohol or drugs.

There were other statistics of note in this same study with regard to assault patterns. In 33% of these cases, the attacker pulled the officer to the ground. In 28% of the cases the attacker pushed them to the ground. In 24% of them, the attacker tackled them. And in 15% of cases, the officer was kicked and punched to the ground.

Once the officer was down, 64% of the time the attacker continued to assault the officer that was taken down. In 31% of cases, the subject fled. And in 5% of cases the subject waited for the officer to get back to their feet to continue the fight. When it

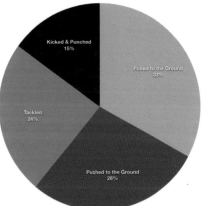

Breakdown of ways police officers were forced to the ground

came to the ground fights, 77% of subjects that continued to fight used grappling and pinning techniques, 66% used strikes, and 21% of them attempted to disarm the officer, with 5% being successful.

As with any statistical information, this must all be kept in context. We must remember that in both of the reports from which the above statistics came, the primary subjects being examined were police officers. In the case of the LAPD report, we must remember that police officers are more likely to willingly go to the ground in order to gain control over their suspect so they could make an arrest. In many of these cases, the officer is likely to have had a partner on scene for back-up, making it safer to do so. The results from the Calibre Press/PPCT Management Systems research project are a little more telling in that they reveal assault patterns for scenarios in which police officers were under attack. These statistics are likely more indicative

---

[*]   As with any statistical information, this must all be kept in context.

of the assault patterns a civilian would experience, but of course there is no way to know for sure.

What we can take away from these statistics is that a significant proportion of fights do indeed end up on the ground, even if it is not likely as high as 80-90%. This, however, does not mean that you would want to willingly go to the ground when you have the choice not to, even if you do have a strong base of ground fighting skills. In most street defense situations, the ground is a dangerous place and the last place you want to be if your goal is self-protection and preservation. Unfortunately, you don't necessarily have the option of picking and choosing the type of physical conflict that you get to deal with. You may be forcefully taken down or knocked down with a strike. You might be attacked when you are already on the ground. Or you may trip and fall in the middle of a standing altercation.

Whatever way you end up there, the ground is a very different type of defensive situation than a stand-up conflict. The skills you have developed for stand-up defense do not necessarily translate to the ground. If your goal in martial arts training is self-protection, it is important to learn skills for defending yourself specifically for this context.

Ground Fighting: Competition vs. Self-Protection

These days when people talk about ground fighting, most often they think of Brazilian Jiu-jitsu (BJJ), as created by the Gracie family. There is no doubt that modern BJJ is one of the most proficient ground grappling systems in the sporting arena. It has become synonymous with the "ground game" of mixed martial arts (MMA). The Ultimate Fighting Championship (UFC) itself was created by the Gracies with the goal of making it a proving ground for their style. In the early days, before people knew what to expect from BJJ, it reigned supreme in these competitions in which different martial arts styles were pitted against each other. Because of this, many people believe that learning to defend one's self on the ground means learning BJJ. It is not as simple as that, however.

In any form of competition, there are rules. This is true even for competitions that try to simulate a real fight like the early UFC contests. Rules are put in place for a variety of reasons; for the competitors' safety, to keep the competition true to a particular style of martial art, to make the fight more exciting for spectators, etc. On the street, in a real attack

Passing the guard scores points in BJJ but may not be the best choice in a street situation

scenario, there are no rules or referees limiting your attacker's or your actions. There is no control over the size or gender of the opponent you must face. There are no special rewards for achieving certain positions or using fancy moves, and people are not likely to let you go if you "tap out." An attacker can and will fight "dirty," and can do anything to get the advantage, whether it means biting, eye gouging, groin attacks, scratching, hair pulling, pinching, or using some sort of weapon.

"There are no rules, only results."
—Professor Georges Sylvain, Founder of Can-ryu Jiu-jitsu

While BJJ may have started out as a self-protection oriented martial art back in the 1920s, it has proliferated in North America as a sport. As a result, the vast majority of BJJ dojos are teaching the style in the context of the submission grappling and MMA as sports. When students train, they usually do so under the confines of the same rules that govern the competitions associated with the style. This means that they don't necessarily learn tactics and skills that are outside of the rules; ones that can help them get the advantage in a street context. Nor do they necessarily learn to protect against someone using such tactics and skills.

Moreover, the goals are quite different in a competitive context as compared to a street context. In competition oriented training, you apply your skills with the goal of earning points, knocking the other person out, or submitting them. In a street context, if your goal is self-protection and self-preservation, you use your skills to stop an attacker by disabling them or hurting them badly enough to make them stop, creating an opportunity for you to escape. Competition rewards engagement. In a street context, however, disengagement, when it can be safely accomplished, is the goal.

That is not to say that sport BJJ or any other form of sport grappling has no place in self-protection. Quite the contrary, the principles of body shifting, weight transference and limb control developed so keenly for sport BJJ, Judo, wrestling, etc, have very practical applications on the street. These skills, in combination with street-oriented tactics and considerations, provide a strong base for self-protection.

The Disadvantages and Dangers of Ground Fighting on the Street

There are a number of potential disadvantages and inherent dangers when it comes to ground fighting in a street context. Anyone interested in self-protection should be aware of them, and they should all be taken into consideration when developing a personal ground defense strategy. Of course, every situation is different and some of these may be more relevant than others depending on the specific situation you find yourself facing.

1. **Size Advantage.** If your attacker is stronger than you and/or outweighs you (which is often the case in a street defense context), he can use his extra strength and weight to a greater advantage when on the ground. It is generally easier for a stronger or larger person to strike, choke, or control their victim. Given two people of equal technique, the person who is bigger and stronger usually dominates. Moreover, size/strength difference by a large margin diminishes the effectiveness of good technique even more so on the ground than it does in a standing position.

2. **Environmental Dangers.** Debris may be strewn about on the ground or floor from which you have to defend yourself. Whether it's broken glass, rocks, a board with a nailing sticking out, or the concrete itself, these things can easily cause injury to you as you fight.

3. **Exposure to Disease.** When you fight from the ground, you are in very close quarters, making you vulnerable to bites and scratches. It can also potentially put you in contact with any open wounds your attacker may have. These factors increase your risk of exposure to communicable diseases.

 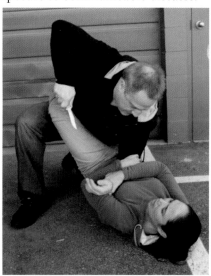

Ground Threat: Multiple Attackers   *Ground Threat: Edged Weapons*

4. **Multiple Attackers.** If your attacker has any cohorts nearby, they can easily deliver potentially fatal kicks to the most vulnerable parts of your body, particularly your head, while you are tied up fighting on the ground with their buddy. This is a common cause of death in street fights.

5. **Edged Weapons.** When you're on the ground, you are more vulnerable to attacks with edged weapons, like knives, which may be concealed on your attacker's person. It is more difficult to defend against such attacks from the ground as it is harder to move quickly, create space, and control the weapon arm.

6. Inability to use physical barriers. In most ground defense situations, you lose the ability to take advantage of any physical barriers the environment may offer. When standing, you're more likely to be able to put things between you and your attacker, like chairs, cars, trash cans, trees, etc., to help you get away.

Legalities Regarding Use of Force

(*Note: The following is **not** legal advice and should not be treated as such. These are only broad guidelines to help you determine how much force might be considered acceptable for you to use to defend yourself in the case of a physical confrontation. Consult your local laws and/or talk to a lawyer to be sure.)

Most countries have a section in their criminal code of sorts intended to present the circumstances under which you are legally justified to defend yourself from a physical assault. The laws are intended to provide the victim legal grounds with which to defend themselves. They also prevent a person who perceives themselves as a victim from using excessive force against an attacker that could have been subdued more humanely. In Canada, this information is presented in Section 34 of the Canadian Criminal Code. In England and Wales, it is presented in section 3 of the Criminal Law Act of 1967 with a further provision about when force is «reasonable» contained in section 76 of the Criminal Justice and Immigration Act 2008. In the United States, the laws can vary from state to state. No matter where you live, it is a good idea to look into what your area's laws are regarding self-defense and use of force, especially if you are training in self-protection skills.

Determining if You are in Imminent Danger of Being Assaulted

Below are a set of questions that you should be prepared to answer for any situation in which you physically defend yourself from an assault. If you can answer "yes" to all these questions, and be able justify these answers, you will be in a better position in which to defend yourself legally if the case ever goes to court:

Did the assailant have or appear to have the ability to physically assault you in the way you perceived?

Did the assailant demonstrate intent? Did his or her words, actions or body language lead you to believe the assailant had the intent of attacking you?

Did the assailant have the means to attack you?

Assailant Factors

In addition to being able to prove that you were in imminent danger of being assaulted when you defended yourself using physical force, the courts are likely to examine additional factors surrounding the assailant when determining the appropriateness of the level of force used. These may include the following:

1. **Age.** Age can play a factor in a number of ways. For example, an elderly person who is confronted with a much younger assailant in the prime of adulthood may need to use a much greater level of force to defend themselves. Conversely, it would be expected that if it were the reverse situation, the able bodied adult should not have to use as much force to defend themselves. Children would also be likely to receive more lenience should they use more force against an adult in an assault.

2. **Size.** This is one of the clearest assailant factors to determine in that all a person needs to do is look at the attacker and defender side by side. Naturally, a relatively small person who encounters a larger assailant may need to use greater levels of force in order to defend themselves successfully.

3. **Gender.** In general, women tend to be both smaller and weaker than men. There are, of course, exceptions, so keep that in mind if you are a six-foot-three female body builder. As a result, a female defender who is assaulted by a male assailant may need to use a greater level of force in order to successfully defend herself.

4. **Skill.** The skill level of the defender and the assailant also enters into determination of acceptable use of force. The defender facing an assailant whose skill level is clearly higher than that of the defender may need to use a higher level of force to defend themselves, and vice versa a defender with decades of martial arts experience may be expected to use exercise greater control and restraint.

5. **Disability.** People with physical disabilities are much more likely to be injured during a physical assault and would likely need to use any means at their disposal in order to successfully defend themselves.

Explanation of the Totality of the Circumstances

In addition to the assailant factors, the courts will look at the big picture of an assault scenario to determine whether the level of force used in response was acceptable.

Imminent Danger: The assailant is known to be armed or has shown themselves to be dangerous in some other intentional way.

Special Knowledge: The assailant is known to have special skills that pose a greater threat.

Injury/Exhaustion. The defender is injured or exhausted.

Multiple Assailants: The defender must face more than one attacker.

Ground Fighting: The defender faces multiple tactical disadvantages (i.e. body weight, debris, communicable disease, weapons, multiple assailants, decreased environmental opportunities.

CHAPTER 2

How to Stay Safe on the Ground

Safety is our primary concern in ground defense training. This is true whether you are developing your skills on the mats or applying them for self-protection in a real street situation. This chapter covers a variety of principles and training practices that will help you learn what you need to stay safe on the ground, while maintaining safety for you and your training partners on the mats.

The Tenets of the Can-ryu Jiu-jitsu Core Curriculum

Before we cover the concepts that are specific to ground defense, it is important to understand the tenets under which we teach the core curriculum of Can-ryu Jiu-jitsu. These serve as guiding principles for what we teach our students for self-protection. These tenets all address the underlying idea that when attacked, people often undergo an adrenaline dump as they face that which threatens them, and that affects the way they move, think, and react.

1. **Simplicity.** Our style's core curriculum is meant to be easy to learn. A student should be able to understand and learn the mechanics of a defensive technique in less than 3 minutes. If there are physiological reasons why a particular move is not practical for a person, the technique should be modified in such a way that it is usable or they should be shown a completely different technique that makes more sense for their body type. But ideally, our core curriculum is formulated to be comprised of techniques that will work for the greatest variety of body types and attack situations. The reason for this is that the harder something is to learn, the less likely we are to use it when under the affects of an adrenaline dump. Of course, the longer you train a technique and commit it to muscle memory, the more likely you are to use it when under attack, but if the technique is easier to learn in the first place, you are that much more likely to develop that tendency.

2. **Commonality of Technique.** We strive to use similar types of techniques in similar defensive situations. The purpose of this is to prevent brain stalls, which can occur under the pressure of an attack as a person tries to "think" of what to do. If the defensive technique that is taught is the same for all the different minor variations of the same attack, it reduces the chances

of this. Also, when you train to defend against all the different variations of a type of attack with the same type of defensive technique, you spend more time committing that technique to muscle memory, making it more likely that you will use it when attacked.

3. **Usage of Gross Motor Skills.** In the interest of making our core curriculum easier to learn and apply, we emphasize the use of gross motor skills over fine motor skills. Gross motor skills are skills that use the larger muscle groups of the body. All gross motor skills come from things we learned from infancy to early childhood, including walking, crawling, maintaining balance, reaching, hopping, etc. By using defensive techniques that employ larger muscle groups, we are drawing on physical skills the body is used to using, ones that have been reinforced since our early physical development. This makes them easier to learn and use when under an adrenaline dump. The body already has a tendency to resort to movements it has already learned, so we are taking advantage of that by using gross motor skills for our defensive techniques. Fine motor skills, on the other hand, require a lot more training to get the movements ingrained in our subconscious minds. That is not to say they cannot be effective (we do include a variety of fine motor skill techniques at higher levels of training in Can-ryu), it just takes longer to develop the muscle memory to make them second nature. Gross motor skills include techniques like open hand strikes, eye gouging, scratching, biting, etc.

4. **Awareness of Additional Threats.** In all the defensive techniques we use in our core curriculum, we emphasize a constant awareness for the potential of additional threats to our safety. This means that we teach students to look around and be aware as though someone else may attack, even when they are defending against one person. This extends into other types of threats that may be actively or passively introduced in a defensive context including weapons and environmental hazards. This is an important skill to develop because our natural tendency is to tunnel-vision when under an adrenaline dump, causing us to focus on what we perceive to be our primary threat. Without training awareness, a person can be vulnerable to changes in circumstances and surroundings when in this psychological state.

The Importance of Making Exceptions

Bear in mind that while these are the guiding principles behind our core curriculum, the defensive techniques we teach may be harder for some people than others based on factors such as size, strength, reach, etc. We must always give ourselves the opportunity to make allowances.

For example, the "3-minute rule" might become the "10-minute rule" if a student is attempting a technique under more challenging circumstances, such as a bigger/heavier training partner. This is especially true for ground defense. They may need the extra time to learn how the mechanics work, and to make them work under more challenging circumstances. This is why it can be beneficial to first try things out with lower levels of resistance on someone who isn't too much bigger. As for commonality of technique, someone may have prior training in a certain way of reacting to a particular attack. Even if it does not necessarily follow with this principle within our style, for self-protection purposes it may make sense for that person to use these previously trained skills because that is the way their body wants to react. When it comes to fine motor skill techniques, they can become equivalent in practical value to ones using gross motor skills when they have been trained enough. When they reach this stage of development, some people may be able to rely upon them as easily as simpler techniques.

When it comes to training and applying techniques for self-protection we try to remember the following maxim: "Never say always. Never say never." There will inevitably be times when we break from the principles, so we must train ourselves to treat each situation as unique and to keep our minds open to alternative solutions.

Ground Defense Rules for Self-Protection

There are four general rules to follow when applying our skills for the purposes of self-protection and preservation:

1. **Rule #1: Protect your head and neck.** If an attacker is trying to immobilize you and eliminate your defensive capabilities, the most dangerous targets are the head and neck. While defending from the ground, you should maintain a protective guard to protect these targets whenever possible. To do this, keep your arms up to form a barrier around your head. Keep

Keeping the head and neck protected

your chin tucked with the shoulders raised to help prevent strikes to the chin and jaw. This also protects against chokes. If being struck, try to keep your head moving to make it harder for your attacker to land a solid blow.

2. **Rule #2: Find/create opportunities.** Like in any defensive situation, you need to find, create and take advantage of defensive opportunities. When fighting from the ground, space is your friend if your goal is to escape. Space opens up more defensive options, allowing you to use more of your body, which is particularly important if your attacker has the size/strength advantage. Attacks to vulnerable targets, in combination with applicable

body shifting techniques, can serve to create more space. The extra space can allow you to use more powerful strikes, apply body shifting more effectively, or simply give you the opportunity to escape.

3. **Rule #3: Keep your limbs close.** If an attacker can get control of your arm or leg, it decreases the number of tools you have to use in defense, also allowing them to more easily apply joint manipulation techniques. When your limbs are fully extended, it is also easier for an attacker to gauge your reach, further minimizing your ability to defend yourself. To keep this from happening, keep your limbs bent and retracted close to your body. This allows you to use your body as an anchor while still being able to use them to attack back.

4. **Rule #4: Get off the ground!** The ground is a dangerous place to be. You greatly increase your ability to protect yourself and escape a conflict by getting off the ground as soon as you have the opportunity to do so safely. As such, it is important to train yourself to get back on our feet once you have escaped a ground attack.

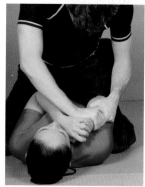

Keep arms close to keep them protected.

Challenges for Different Body Types

There is no "one size fits all" approach to ground defense. Differences in height, weight, and body type create different challenges for each person when it comes to ground defense techniques. The challenges also change depending on the size and body type of your attacker. Different techniques work better for different people. While in this book, we strive to present techniques that will work best for the widest range of people, inevitably there are exceptions that may necessitate an

Every body type has different challenges

altered approach. Or you may find advantages that are unique to you that serve to improve your defensive capabilities on the ground. Whatever the situation, experiment and improvise using the materials in this book and any other useful resources to find what works best for your unique body type.

1. **Petite Bodies.** If you're this body type, you are usually shorter, lighter, and weaker than the average attacker (for the purposes of this book, we assume that the average attacker is a man). Because your legs and arms are shorter, you are able to strike more effectively and move more freely when your limbs are not immobilized. If you try to use strength to fight strength, you will tire out quickly, making yourself less capable of mounting an effective defense. If you're fully pinned and there is not an immediate and/or urgent need to escape, you may want to wait for opportunities in which you have more freedom of movement rather than fighting hard in a scenario that will exhaust you.

2. **Tall and Lanky Bodies.** If you're this body type, may find it more difficult to use your limbs strategically because they tend to be longer and harder to manuever in the confines of certain types of ground defense situations. You'll likely need to use strikes to create more space so that you can more effectively use your body. Fortunately, when you have the space, the extra reach that your body type affords can make it easier to access targets that are farther away.

3. **Big and Broad Bodies.** If you're this body type, you probably won't find ground defense very challenging when facing an average sized man without a skill advantage. You may not have the speed and flexibility that other body types are more likely to have, but you are more likely to be able to make up for that with mass and strength. Because of your breadth, you can more easily off-balance an attacker that is on top of you without using much strength. This is an ability that you should develop in your training whenever possible. Practice your ground defense skills against people who are closer to your own size (or bigger) whenever possible for the purposes of realism as this is more likely going to be situation on the street.

Safety Practices in Training

While we want to create as realistic an environment as practical when training, it is important to do so and still maintain the safety of all participants. No one wants to get an injury that will keep them from training whether it's a small cut that interrupts their class in order to receive first aid, or a more serious joint injury that can keep them away for months. As such, we encourage everyone to follow the practices below to keep everyone safe.

1. **Tap early, tap often.** If your partner achieves a strong submission position, don't delay in tapping in the hopes of muscling your way out. If they have superior positioning, you risk injury by trying to force your way out. The best way to tap is to tap the person's body, or if that is not possible, you can tap the mat very loudly. If tapping is impossible, or simply not fast enough, you can do so verbally by saying, "Tap!" or "Stop!"

2. **Stay relaxed and avoid using strength.** When tousling on the ground, the tendency for an untrained person is to use frantic movements to fight the person off. This tendency should be avoided in training. Staying relaxed and avoiding the use of strength helps you conserve energy, makes you harder to move, helps you to see more opportunities, and keeps everyone safer as they train in ground defense. While this is a general training rule, and in a real self-protection scenario, there may be cases in which using frantic kicks with less abandon, what we call "going alley cat crazy," in a forceful, all-out defense makes sense, particularly when the defender has little to no ground defense training (a concept we regularly teach in our women's self-defense courses).

3. **Have fun and check macho attitudes at the door.** Your training partner is your friend and is there to help you learn. Failing to get out of a hold or being tapped out is educational and will make you a better martial artist. Embrace these experiences and actively try to learn from them by asking questions and striving to improve your defensive capabilities. Having too much ego keeps you from learning and having fun.

4. **Wear protective equipment.** When training in self-defense oriented ground combat, the groin is an often used target. In order to train strikes to the groin realistically and safely, students, both men and women, should wear groin protectors. When doing more live training drills, wearing a mouth guard is also a good idea for preventing incidental damage to mouth area and for absorbing some of the shock of accidental blows to the head/jaw.

5. **Keep your nails trimmed.** Finger and toe nails can cause nasty cuts and gashes when doing ground defense training. Breaking a nail can also be quite painful. You should always keep your finger and toe nails trimmed and filed. A freshly cut nail that isn't filed can be just as dangerous as a long nail.

6. **Maintain good hygiene.** While this may seem obvious, not everyone realizes how far they have to go for training safety and comfort. Keep your body sensibly clean and keep your B.O. under control. Pay particular attention to the cleanliness of feet because you are in closer proximity of them during ground defense training. If you eat strong foods, brush your teeth or use a mouthwash/breath freshener before training. Lastly, keep your uniform clean. Don't just leave it in your bag after a sweaty session. The next time you open your bag, the smell will be appalling. If you had a light session, you might be able to get away with just hanging your uniform up to air out, but most of the time, you should be washing it.

7. **Don't train sick or when suffering from an infection.** There is a lot of body contact in ground defense and if you're sick, there is a good chance you'll pass on your illness to others. You're also more likely to tire yourself out and make mistakes that can cause injuries when you're not in good health. It is also very important not to go on the mats if you have a skin infection

like ringworm or staph. They are highly contagious and easily spread from person to person or from person to mat to person.

Live Training as a Learning Tool

When you first start training in ground defense, you usually stick to choreographed attacks and defenses giving you more opportunities to develop your skills and techniques. Eventually though, you'll need to move on from this style of training and apply what you have learned in a more "live" training environment. Ground fighting can be fast and dynamic. Things can change very quickly on the ground, and if you're not trained to adapt quickly, you may find yourself helpless on the ground if someone gets the jump on you.

Whether you do live training with a partner or in a training circle, you can train at different levels of intensity depending on whether you want to improve your technical applications or increase the difficulty level and realism of the exercise. I like to work with three different levels of intensity with my students, which are as follows:

Level #1: The attacking partner sticks to a single hold down (no striking is allowed). The attacker may resist the defender's attempts to escape if ineffective, but must always return to their original attack rather than changing their attack. The attacker should loosen up or respond appropriately to the defender's attacks to vital targets without changing their attack. This style of live training is designed to increase technical understanding and confidence with defensive techniques.

Level #2: Punching attacks are allowed and hold-downs are done with higher intensity. Defenders should strive to get back to their feet within 10 seconds of the start of the attack. If the defender fails to get to their feet, the attacker may change their method of attack. The attacker should still loosen up or respond appropriately to the defender's vital target attacks without changing their attack. When attacking with punches, use appropriate protective equipment such as mouth guards and gloves. As an alternative to using gloves, light open hand strikes to non-injurious areas may be used. Whichever method you use, the attacker should strike at a power level that is safe for training. Not even MMA fighters spar at full power and intensity for safety reasons. You don't need to in order to develop your skills. This style of live training is designed to give you a higher level of realism to help you apply your skills under greater pressure.

Level #3: Attackers may change their strategy based on the type of defense used by the defender. A higher level of intensity may be used. The attacker may take measures to resist the defender's vital target attacks, but still responding appropriately if the defender lands a vital target strike. Again, defenders should still strive to get back to their feet within 10 seconds.

Live Sport-Oriented Ground Grappling as a Training Tool

Even if you have no interest in competitions or tournaments, it is worthwhile to train in sport-oriented ground grappling. There are more and more people training in BJJ and MMA these days and not all of them necessarily do so with honest intentions. If you want to be able to handle skilled sport grapplers in a self-protection scenario, you need to understand what they do. The best way to do that is to train in it. This will make you and your training partners better at playing that type of attacker, which makes you all better at dealing with it.

Here are a variety of ways to train in live sport-oriented ground grappling:

- Working with a partner, one person tries to maintain a particular top position. The defender uses body-shifting techniques alone to get into a more defensible position. Once this has been achieved or a time limit is reached, switch roles. As you get better, the person on top can transition between positions to make the exercise more difficult.
- Working with a partner, one person works from a particular position and try to either improve their position or apply a submission. The defender uses body-shifting techniques to get into a more defensible position. Once the attacker has improved their position or achieved a submission, or a time limit is reached, switch roles.
- Simply shake hands with a partner and perform free grappling from a kneeling position, or standing position as you gain more experience. Some days you'll be full of energy and might welcome a vigorous "roll." Other days you might be feeling a bit off, mentally or physically. Be sure to work at an appropriate intensity level. If your partner is going faster and harder than you are comfortable with, communicate that and ask them to ease off a bit.

Addressing Size Differences in Training

When you train ground defense in class, you'll inevitably end up training with people with whom there is a significant size difference. If students don't approach these situations with the right attitude, one might them frustrating while the other student finds them boring. Here are suggestions you can make to help get the most out of these pair-ups:

For the Larger of the Pair

If you're working on self-protection techniques, you have to approach your training creatively. Obviously a much smaller person is highly unlikely to attack you and grapple you on the ground. Of course, if you are a very large person, you'll probably find fewer people who would make a "realistic" attacker for you. Make the most of your training by seeing how smaller people need to move to handle your greater size.

When you're practicing your own defenses, do your best to relax, take all your strength out of the equation, and work on technique. If you're doing more sport oriented grappling, focus on developing better positional strategy and improving the technical application of your submissions. Of course your weight will still give you an edge if you're doing what you are supposed to in terms of positional strategy. No matter what type of ground defense you're working on, whether it is escaping holds, applying submissions, or doing positional transitions, try not to just muscle your way through. This leads to a much greater risk that you could accidentally injure your much smaller partner, plus you really don't improve your ground defense skills from the experience.

When you're playing the role of attacker, be sure to play fair and respond appropriately to strikes that would have been effectively applied had your partner used full power. You do not want them to escalate the level of force unsafely just to make it work.

For the Smaller of the Pair

When training in self-protection oriented ground defense, keep your training practices safe. Sometimes a larger training partner doesn't realize that they aren't responding appropriately to your vital target attacks. If that is the case, try to make the strike more obvious, but don't escalate the force to an unsafe level. If all else fails, communicate with your partner or get your instructor's help to deal with the situation.

While sport oriented grappling is a lot of fun, you must be aware that you are at a physical disadvantage when you train with much larger partners. That is not to say there is no value in doing it; you just have to keep it in context. If the larger person you're grappling is of equal or greater skill, you're not as likely to tap them out (though if the opportunity presents itself, of course, attempt it). Instead, focus on developing your defensive strategies. Because you're smaller, your technical defense must be that much better to make up the difference. You can also agree to different rules in which you are allowed to use certain types of pressure attacks to help create openings to make up for your lack of size. Be sure to communicate with your partner as you grapple. Tap early and tap often, especially if you find they're over-relying on strength. You will probably lose a strength battle if it comes down to it, and it is not worth risking injury. If you're more skilled than the person you're grappling with, help your partner with their technique. Stop the action when you see that they're using strength and show them a more technical option. People often use strength simply because they don't know any better, so it is in both your interests if you help him or her.

CHAPTER 3

Primary Tools for Ground Defense—Body Shifting and Control

In this chapter, you'll learn the general use of body shifting techniques and dominant position strategy. This, in combination with attacks to vital targets (see Chapter 4), comprises the primary tools for ground defense. If you have a martial arts background, some of it may already be familiar to you. These tools are diverse and can have a wide variety of applications, so many that it is impossible to include them all in this book. That being said, by knowing a good base of the many tools available to you, you can easily learn to use and apply them for self-protection in a way that makes sense for you.

This book contains a number of chapters showing methods of applying these tools in a variety of ground defense situations. Consider these as a base for learning and training in their use. As you become more skilled in their application, you'll discover different ways of using them beyond what you read about in this book. You may also learn techniques from different sources, which can be incorporated into the way you defend yourself. All of this is important for developing your own personal adaptive ground defense system. Once you have become comfortable with the basics, it is important to move beyond set, formulaic attacks and learn to apply these tools against a live, adaptive attacker. See "Live Training as a Learning Tool" in Chapter 2 for more details.

Body Shifting

Body shifting techniques are a vital tool for finding and/or creating defensive opportunities when you're on the ground. They can put you in a better position to attack vital targets more effectively. They can also put you or keep you in a more defensive position. The body shifting techniques shown here are adaptive and can be combined strategically depending on how an attacker changes his method of attack. These exercises are great for developing technique and can also be used as warm-up drills for ground defense training.

Keeping Your Legs between You and Your Attacker

This type of body shifting is for use when you're down on the ground and your attacker is standing. When you're in this position, your legs offer you the strongest tools for self-protection. Therefore, the greatest threat to you in this position is if the attacker is able to get around your legs, whether it's so they kick your head or get on top of you. The goal of this body shifting technique is to keep this from happening.

1. When your attacker is facing you directly, stay flat on your back facing them with your legs directly between you. Keep both legs bent to make it harder for him to determine your reach *(Figure 3.1)*.

2. If the attacker tries to move past your legs, lift your hips and reposition your body to maintain your original position *(Figure 3.2–3.3)*.

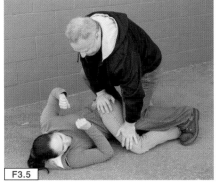

3. If the attacker tries to move more quickly around your legs, shift your weight on to your side. To keep your legs between you and your attacker, lift your body to minimize drag and walk with your legs, keeping your legs uncrossed *(Figure 3.4)*. This keeps the attacker from taking control of your legs by pinning them together *(Figure 3.5)*.

4. If an attacker breaks into a run to get around your legs to kick your head, you will need to move more quickly to prevent this from happening. If it is clear that the attacker has committed to an attempt to kick your head, their focus is not on trying to control your legs. This means that you can cross one over the other to turn your body more quickly *(Figure 3.6)*.

F3.6

F3.7

F3.8

5. If an attacker changes direction suddenly, they may be able get past your legs on the other side. To prevent this, push off the ground using your elbow and aggressively roll your body to your other side *(Figure 3.7–3.8)*.

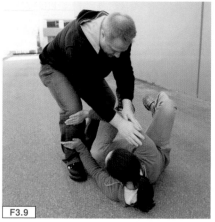

F3.9

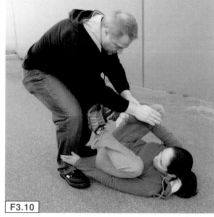

F3.10

6. If an attacker manages to get around your legs, he may try to mount you. As he comes around your legs, place one or both of your hands on one of his legs (one if you are on your back, two if on your side) *(Figure 3.9)*. Push off the leg, using the attacker's weight and momentum for leverage, lifting your hips up over their leg. This re-establishes your defensive position allowing you to kick at will *(Figure 3.10–3.12)*.

Bridging and Rolling

Bridging and rolling is an important tool for when an attacker is mounted on the front of your body in some way. The goal is to aggressively upset the balance of the attacker so that they have to redistribute their weight in order to stay on top. This opens up greater opportunities to strike and/or escape the mount and other positions. When done repetitively, this exercise is good for developing technique while strengthening muscles throughout your body, including your abdominals, back, legs, and buttocks.

1. Start on your back with your legs bent and your hands up *(Figure 3.13)*.
2. Pushing into the ground with the balls of your feet, bridge your hips up explosively leaning on to your left shoulder *(Figure 3.14–13.15)*.

3. Pass your left leg behind the right and roll over into a plank position with the body straight supported by your forearms and the balls of your feet.

4. Return to the starting position by passing your left arm behind your right arm and rolling on to your left shoulder *(Figure 3.17–3.19)*.

5. Pass your left leg behind your right, turning your body back up into the bridged position *(Figure 3.20–3.21)*.
6. Lower your hips to reset. Repeat this movement on the right.

Shrimping

Shrimping is another important tool for ground defense. It can be used to disrupt the balance of a mounted attacker by turning on to your hips, which in turn creates an opening for escape or space with which to improve your defensive position. It can also be used simply to reposition your body into a more defensive position. When done repetitively, this exercise is good for developing technique while strengthening your abdominal muscles.

1. Start on your back with your legs bent and your hands up *(Figure 3.22)*.

2. Pushing into the ground with the balls of your feet, lift your hips up slightly.

3. While continuing to push with your feet, turn your body over on to its side thrusting your hips back as you push your hands toward your feet as though pushing on your attacker for leverage *(Figure 3.25–3.26)*. Repeat on the other side.

Turtling

Turtling is an important tool for when an attacker is attacking you from the rear while you are on your stomach. The goal is to get one or both elbows and/or one or both knees under your body. By putting your elbow under your shoulder or your knee under your hips, you're able to get more leverage with less effort. This allows you to upset your attacker's balance and/or improve your defensive position. When done repetitively, this exercise is good for developing technique while strengthening your back muscles.

F3.27

1. Start on your belly with your arms and legs out.

F3.28

F3.29

2. Explosively bring both elbows under your shoulders. Return to starting position.
3. Explosively bring both knees under your hips. Return to starting position.

F3.30

F3.31

4. Explosively bring your right elbow under your shoulder and your left knee under your hip. Return to starting position. Repeat with the opposite limbs. Return to starting position *(Figure 3.30)*.
5. Explosively bring both arms under your shoulders and both legs under your hips. Return to starting position *(Figure 3.31)*.

Dominant Position Strategy

While less important for self-protection when your goal is escape, there are still good reasons for training in dominant ground positions. If you work in law enforcement, you may find yourself on the ground trying to control a suspect. Even if you don't, you'll become more effective at defending against dominant positions if you understand how they are applied. Plus, if you and your training partners all train in these positions you'll hone your defensive skills against attackers with a higher level of skill. As the primary goal of this book is escape, the opportunities for attack and control from the dominant positions is provided for training purposes.

When practicing dominant positions, start by taking the position with a compliant partner, getting feedback to help get the best weight distribution. Once you're fully in position, you can have your partner resist and try to break from beneath you. This allows you to practice shifting your weight to keep it in the ideal position.

Full Mount

The mount position is psychologically intimidating, and can be physically exhausting for the person on the bottom. It also allows the attacker to strike the head and set up a variety of submissions. There are two common ways of doing a full mount, postured up and chest down.

Postured Up

The postured up version is dynamic and allows you to "ride" the person beneath you more easily, especially if you're seated higher up on the chest. You can post with your arms and sprawl with your legs and quickly retract them in from this position. You also have the opportunity to strike to the head.

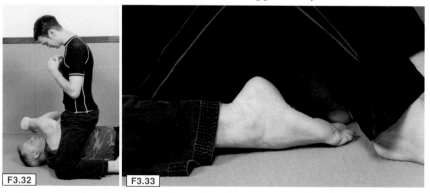

Keep your hands up out of reach when not engaging in submissions or strikes *(Figure 3.32)*. Keep the tops of your feet on the ground rather than the balls of your feet to protect your ankles if you get rolled *(Figure 3.33)*.

Chest Down

Putting the weight of your chest down on to the person below when in mount has its purposes. You may do this to gain greater control for submissions, or to transition to a side control position. Or if you're a larger individual, you might use this position to smother the defender and/or tire them out.

Hook the defender's legs with your own legs, stretching them out as widely as possible to make it difficult for them to bridge and roll *(Figure 3.34)*. Grab your own wrist around the defender's head and shoulder, while maintaining even distribution of weight on the defender's chest and hips *(Figure 3.35)*.

Scarf Hold

This position is great for control and is popular in submission grappling sports. When used well, it can be difficult to escape and a good choice for tiring out the defender. There is, however, less variety in the types of submissions you can use directly from this position.

Wrap your close arm around the opposite side of the defender's neck while securing their inside arm with your outside arm. You can secure the hold further by grabbing the defender's arm/sleeve or your own leg with the hand of the arm that is controlling the neck and shoulders *(Figure 3.36)*.

Most people teach students to keep their hips on the ground, holding them tightly into the defender's body. I teach this a little differently. If you keep your hips slightly lifted, you can shift more of your body weight into the defender making it harder for the defender to breathe and more effort to move *(Figure 3.37)*. When using this method, center your body weight on the sternum (center of the chest) and keep the legs wide for stability. The knee of the outside leg should be pointed up with your foot planted. As the defender tries to displace your weight one way or the other, use your legs to shift your own weight one way or the other to counter. This method of doing the scarf hold has worked better for me being a smaller person who has to grapple with people who are bigger and stronger than me. It allows you to use more of your weight to pin down and control the defender. It does, however, require a greater level of sensitivity to your defender's movements. As with anything, use whatever works best for you.

Side Control

There are two common side control positions, with either one knee in or both knees in. Having both legs out leaves no opportunity for you to control the defender's hips, so it isn't as useful. These side control positions are good for tiring out the defender while having the opportunity to switch into other dominant positions easily as necessary. A number of submissions are also possible from this position.

One Knee In

F3.38

This type of side control is often preferred by people who have smaller, lighter builds as it allows you to put more of your body weight onto the defender's chest.

Keep your legs wide for stability and your hips a little higher than your chest *(Figure 3.38)*. Use your outstretched leg to pitch your weight forward into the defender's chest. Control your defender's hips using the elbow and knee closest to them. Keep the other arm behind the head, either hand flat on the ground or grabbing the collar or opposite shoulder.

Both Knees In

This type of side control is often preferred by people who are broader as their build allows the defender less space to move.

Sink as much weight as you can into their chest through your body, rather than resting your weight fully on your arms and legs. Underhooking the defender's arm with your arm, clasping your hands in a gable grip gives you greater control of the upper body.

F3.39

Reverse Scarf Hold

This position is often used as a transitional position and can help you keep more control over the defender as you move into the mount from a scarf hold. It is also good for maintaining control while keeping an eye on what the defender is doing to escape.

F3.40

F3.41

As with the standard scarf hold, keep the hips slightly lifted, sinking your body weight into the defender's sternum. Do this with the side of your body, not with your back as this makes you vulnerable to attacks from the rear such as the rear naked choke. Keep control of the arms if possible.

Knee-On-Belly

This position is great if you want to control your opponent and still have the opportunity to get to your feet quickly if necessary, making it useful for law enforcement purposes. The defender may find it hard to breathe as you sink most of your weight into their solar plexus through your knee and shin. You also have the opportunity to

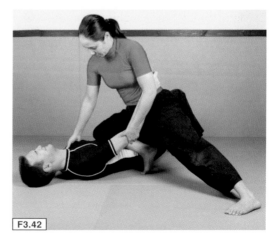

F3.42

strike to the head from this position, or use submissions. Please note that knee-on-belly is an advanced position and requires some flexibility to maintain it effectively. *(Figure 3.42)*

Keep your inside foot's heel up to pitch more of your weight into the defender's solar plexus through your knee and shin. This foot can also be used to hook the body for stability as the defender tries to displace your weight. Your outside leg is kept sprawled wide for stability. Use your close hand to grip the defender's clothing or secure it behind their neck while your opposite arm controls their closest arm.

Flow Drill for Training Dominant Positions

One of the keys to being good at staying on top of a defender is being able to transition to other positions without losing control of the person. To do this, you must learn to keep your weight on the defender consistently without a break as you flow from one position to another. Any time your weight comes off, there is a greater chance the person will be able get out from under you or improve their defensive position. This drill allows you to practice transitions. To get the most out of it, start slowly without resistance, focusing on weight distribution. Then add speed followed by resistance to further develop your skill with dominant positions.

F3.43

F3.44

1. Start in one of the side control positions, whichever you prefer *(Figure 3.43)*.
2. Maintaining your weight centered on the sternum, turn your body toward the left into the scarf hold. Keep your hips up as you shift or the weight will come off the sternum *(Figure 3.44)*.

F3.45

F3.46

3. Settle into a solid scarf hold *(Figure 3.45–3.46)*.

4. Maintaining your weight on the sternum, rotate your body toward the left into the reverse scarf hold. Again, keep the hips up as you shift *(Figure 3.47)*.

5. Settle into a solid reverse scarf hold *(Figure 3.48)*.

6. Using your right hand grab your partner's left leg and draw both legs toward you *(Figure 3.49)*.

7. Keeping your weight on the chest, leading with your knee, bring your right leg across to the other side of your partner's body. This must be done as tightly as possible, keeping your foot away from your partner's legs to avoid getting stuck in a half-guard *(Figure 3.50)*.

8. Establish a solid full mount, whichever version you prefer *(Figure 3.51–3.52)*.

9. To transition to side control on the opposite side, sink your weight into your partner's chest and bring your right arm around the head. Leading

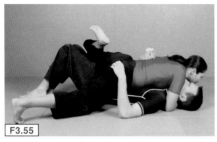

F3.55

F3.56

with your left foot, draw your leg through to the opposite side of your partner's body. Do this as tightly as possible, keeping your foot away from your partner's legs to avoid getting stuck in a half-guard. Establish a solid side control position. Repeat this sequence on the opposite side *(Figure 3.53–3.56)*.

Special Tips for Law Enforcement Officers

The tools and techniques in this book are useful for you if you're a law enforcement officer, though it is important to bear in mind that you have special considerations that are different from that of civilians. Since you carry a "tool belt" containing weapons you need to be aware of your different advantages and disadvantages. If a suspect grapples you on the ground, reports state that there is a one in five chance that they will attempt to disarm you, so protecting your weapons is of primary importance to you. Fortunately, you may also have the opportunity to use a weapon against your suspect. For example, if you have fallen, you may be able to act fast and draw your pistol before the suspect tries to engage you on the ground. This, in combination with vocal assertiveness, may be enough to stop the suspect in their tracks.

Other than being disarmed, you need to also consider how your tool belt will affect your movement on the ground. Certain body shifting techniques will require modification. When keeping your legs between you and your attacker, you'll likely need to do all your body shifting from flat on your back, as your tools will get in the way if you try to move onto your weapon side. You may need to do shrimping only on one side to prevent your tools from getting in the way of your movement.

F3.57

As a law enforcement officer, you may want to also spend extra time learning to control people with your body weight on the ground from dominant positions. Positions like the knee-on-belly offer a great amount of control, while giving you the option to easily get to your feet, access your weapons and respond to other threats if necessary.

F3.58

To make your training more specifically applicable to what you do, try training your ground defense wearing everything that you would normally wear as part of your job, including full uniform, body armor, boots, tool belt, etc. Since each agency's standard issue is different and not every officer carries the same tools, you may find you need to make adjustments to techniques to make them work best for you.

F3.59

CHAPTER 4

Primary Tools for Ground Defense—Attacks to Vital Targets

While body shifting techniques are great tools, on their own they may not be enough to successfully defend against a much larger attacker. Attacks to vital targets serve to create defensive opportunities, whether it is by distracting the attacker with pain or discomfort (or the threat thereof) or by opening up more space to make it easier to use body shifting techniques or more powerful strikes. There are targets all over the head, body, arms and legs. The more aware you are of potential targets and the different ways to attack them, the more likely you are to reflexively use them as your defensive situation changes over the course of an attack.

Keep in mind that attacks to vital targets that only cause pain, such as nerve pressure points, may not be enough against a pain-resistant attacker (i.e. someone who is drunk, high, enraged, etc). In such cases, you're better off using strikes that create space and open up opportunities for body shifting techniques or more powerful strikes. Either way, always be prepared for the possibility that a strike may not have the desired effect, whether the attacker is tolerant to pain or simply is able to defend against it successfully. Always be ready to follow up with other attacks to other targets and/or body shifting techniques.

Head Targets

Eyes

Almost any type of attack to the eyes will cause a reaction, whether it's as a result of pain or a reflexive flinch to protect the eyes. Note: The eyes are considered a dangerous target in that it could cause a permanent injury that could severely affect one's livelihood in the long term. It is important to not only be justified in such an attack, but to be able to articulate why you did it. Loren Christensen points out in his book, *Fighting the Pain Resistant Attacker*, that you should be able to explain that with a combination of the following points:

- Your pain-based techniques didn't stop him.
- He was continuing to assault you.
- At that precise moment, his eyes were the only target available that you thought would get a reaction.
- Your intent was not to cause permanent damage but to distract him so you could flee.

Methods of Attack

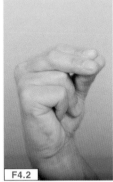

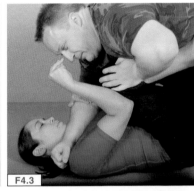

1. Strike with a reinforced thumb *(Figure 4.1)*.
2. Strike with reinforced fingers *(Figure 4.2–4.3)*.
3. Apply pressure with thumb *(Figure 4.4)*.

4. Flick your fingers across eyes from bottom to top, dragging your nails. Or it could simply be used to cause the person to flinch away without even making any contact *(Figure 4.5–4.6)*.

5. Scratch across the face in the area of the eyes. The goal is not to scratch the person's eyes, but any of the sensitive skin surrounding the eyes (i.e. the upper and lower lids). Similar to the flick, it can also be used to cause the person to flinch away without even making any contact.

Nose

A hard strike to the nose causes most people great pain, even if it doesn't break. It can also cause the tear ducts to empty out, making it hard to see. Even just strong pressure can be enough to cause pain to the cross-section of nerves that are there.

Methods of Attack

F4.7 F4.8

1. Strike with your palm. This is one of the easiest, most common ways to strike the nose *(Figure 4.7)*.
2. Apply pressure with the base of your palm, wiggling the nose back and forth. This can be used when the attacker is too close to use a strike.
3. Strike using your elbows. This can be done towards the front or rear, depending on your position *(Figure 4.8)*.

Skull

The back of the skull is one of the most dangerous targets. A strong blow can stun a person and cause them to lose consciousness. It also has the potential to cause a person to go into a coma, lose their sight, or it could even kill them. These extremes are less likely to happen when defending yourself from the ground since you aren't able to generate as much power due to your compromised position. That being said, you should be able to justify the need to strike this target based on the threat you faced and the circumstances surrounding it. There are other, less dangerous options when striking the skull if the threat is not as serious.

Methods of Attack

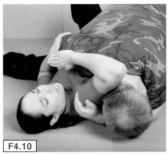

F4.9   F4.10   F4.11

1. Open palm strike to the back of the skull. Use the whole hand (palm and flats of fingers) to get the best distribution for an increased concussive effect.
2. Elbow to the back of the skull. Use the flat part of your elbow to get the best distribution for an increased concussive effect *(Figure 4.10)*.
3. Knuckle strikes to the skull. The goal is to cause pain to distract your attacker. This can be applied to any part of the skull *(Figure 4.11)*.

Throat/Jugular Notch

The throat is one of the most dangerous targets. A strong blow to the frontal throat area can damage the thyroid, Adam's apple, even crush the windpipe, cricoid cartilage or damage the laryngeal nerves, potentially lead to suffocation and death. If you're going to use a strike of any kind, you should be able to justify the need to strike this target based on the circumstances surrounding it. Another way to attack the throat is using the jugular notch as a pressure point. It causes discomfort and oftentimes a gag reflex. This is less dangerous than using strikes and can be used to create distance.

Methods of Attack

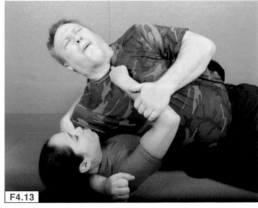

F4.12   F4.13

1. Tiger mouth strike to throat. This is a potentially lethal way to strike the throat. Use appropriately *(Figure 4.12)*.

2. Finger pressure to the jugular notch. Reinforce your middle finger on top of your index and push in and down on the jugular notch *(Figure 4.13)*.

Hair

Depending on your attacker, the hair can be a great way to manipulate their weight distribution, create space, and/or cause distracting pain. It may not be appropriate, however, if the attacker is bald, has very short hair, or a high tolerance that type of pain.

Methods of Attack

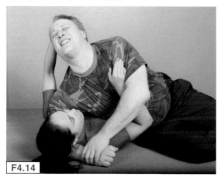 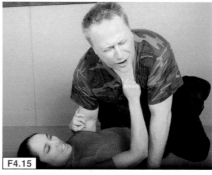

F4.14   F4.15

1. Pull hair on head. To get the best leverage, grab a fistful of hair from the top of the head (as close to the roots as possible for maximum pain and control) and pull back *(Figure 4.14)*.
2. Rip out hair on chest. If your attacker has a hairy chest, one option may be to grab a fist full of this hair, twist and pull sharply. The skin in this area can be sensitive, so ripping the hair out of this area can cause quite a bit of pain *(Figure 4.15)*.

Ears

A solid blow to the eardrum causes trauma to the area, which can cause pain, dizziness, loss of balance, and loss of hearing. The strike may cause damage to the ligaments, muscles and nerves of the neck due to impact. This type of damage is less likely to happen when defending yourself from the ground since you aren't able to generate as much power due to your compromised position. That being said, due to the type of dangers associated with a strike to the eardrum, you should be able to justify using it based on the threat you faced and the circumstances surrounding it. Attacking the outer ear (i.e. the skin and cartilage) is much less dangerous, but only causes pain, which means it may not be effective against a pain-resistant attacker.

Methods of Attack

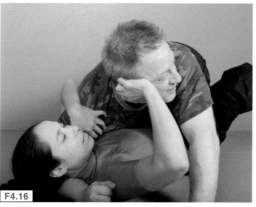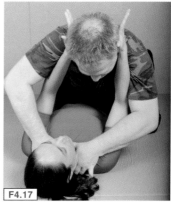

1. Grab and pull the outer ear. The skin and cartilage of the outer ear can be quite sensitive.
2. Palm strike to one or both ears. Use cupped palms to create a vacuum in the inner ear on impact, causing pain and potential damage to the eardrum.

Lower Jaw

Striking the lower jaw can cause a mild concussion and/or unconsciousness. This happens because the jaw bone can act as a lever to transmit the force of a strike to the back of the brain where cardiac and respiratory functions are controlled. While the potential effects are less serious than those of a strike to the back of the skull, you still need to justify the need to strike this target based on the threat you faced and the circumstances surrounding it. Attacking the mandibular angle, a nerve pressure point, is much less dangerous because it only causes pain and can be used to create distance. That being said, it may not be effective against a pain-resistant attacker.

Methods of Attack

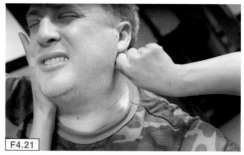

1. Palm strike under chin. Curl your fingers and thumb back to expose the palm for this strike *(Figure 4.18)*.
2. Forward elbow strike to outside lower jaw. Using the end of the elbow makes this strike more effective *(Figure 4.19)*.
3. Backward elbow strike. Can be used if the attacker is on the outside of your arm. Again, using the end of the elbow is more effective *(Figure 4.20)*.
4. Thumb compression to mandibular angle. Anchor your thumb to the knuckle of your index finger. Apply pressure with the tip of your thumb behind the jaw toward the eye on the opposite side of the head. Hold the other side of the head with your hand for more leverage *(Figure 4.21)*.

Torso Targets

Groin

The groin is often a good target on the ground because it doesn't take much force to cause a reaction. Just the threat of a strike to the groin can be enough to make an attacker shift his hips away to defend. Some attackers will experience great pain when their groin is attacked; men who are pain-resistant for whatever reason, may not react. Many people operate on the assumption that if you can get in a good attack to the groin, you're done. Don't assume this will always be the case. Always be prepared to follow up with alternatives.

Methods of Attack

1. Finger whip. When you use this type of attack, essentially you are doing an open hand strike to the groin, allowing your fingers to whip around to better access the testicles *(Figure 4.22)*.
2. Grab and squeeze. This attack can be used when there is no space to complete a strike. Simply grab the testicles, squeeze and give a little twist *(Figure 4.23)*.

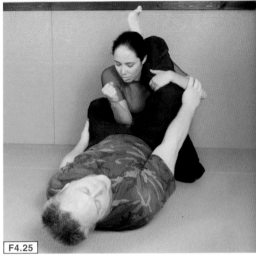

3. Kick. When the attacker is on his feet or knees and you have some distance, you kick the groin using either the heel or the ball of the foot *(Figure 4.24)*.

4. Elbow drop. If you get tied up in your attacker's legs, an elbow strike can be an effective way of getting loose *(Figure 4.25)*.

Ribs

The floating ribs are the two lowermost pairs of ribs of the rib cage. They are called "floating" because they are attached to the vertebrae only and not to the sternum or cartilage coming off the sternum. Because they lack this extra support, they are vulnerable to strikes. Striking them can cause pain, severe bruising or breakage. Another way to attack the rib area is to target the lateral thoracic, a nerve pressure point that encompasses all the intercostal nerves that lie between the ribs. This target is appropriate for lower risk situations, but be mindful of the fact that because it is a purely a pain-based attack, it may not work on attackers that are pain-resistant for whatever reason.

Methods of Attack

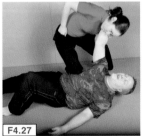

1. Elbow strike to floating ribs. Use the point of your elbow to strike the floating ribs sharply *(Figure 4.26)*.

2. Knee drop to floating ribs. You may want to use this if you have taken a person to the ground and your attacker is trying to pull you down. A sharp blow would have the strongest effects. You can also simply drop your weight through your knee to compress the floating ribs into the solar plexus, causing a winding effect *(Figure 4.27)*. (See below for more info on the solar plexus.)

3. Knuckle compression to the lateral thoracic. Protrude the middle knuckle within a secure fist. Use this knuckle to rake across the ribs to compress the intercostal nerves against the rib bones. If possible, hold the other side of the body with your hand for more leverage *(Figure 4.28)*.

Solar Plexus

The solar plexus is nerve motor point that consists of a complex network of nerves located behind the stomach below the pectoral muscles. A solid blow causes pain for some and motor dysfunction to the muscles that control breathing, resulting temporarily in difficulty breathing. To get enough power to affect this target on the ground, you'll need to resort to kicks or strikes that allow you to put your body weight behind them. Bear in mind that striking this area may not be effective against some individuals.

Methods of Attack

F4.29

F4.30

1. Kick. Once you've created enough space from your attacker, you may have the opportunity to use a turtle kick or side kick *(Figure 4.29)*.

2. Elbow drop. If someone is trying to draw you down in their guard, an elbow drop can be used to gain release. Tuck your elbow in close to your center to make it easier to drop your body weight into the strike *(Figure 4.30)*.

Sensitive Skin Areas

Certain areas of skin on the torso are more sensitive than others, including the nipple region and the area on the sides of the body commonly referred to as "love handles." Attacking these areas can cause great pain in some people, but may not have any effect on a pain-resistant attacker. (When biting bare skin, there is a chance you could break the skin and expose yourself to any communicable diseases your attacker may have. You may prefer to use a different type of attack if you have the option, but if the stakes are high and your options limited, biting may be preferable.)

Methods of Attack

1. Bite to the nipple. There are certain occasions in which an attacker may hold your head close into his chest. This is a good opportunity to use a bite to the sensitive skin surrounding the nipple. Bite down sharply then shake your head from side to side while growling loudly. The psychological effect of this can be more powerful than the actual pain *(Figure 4.31)*.

F4.31

2. Grab and squeeze love handles. When engaged in ground defense, there are times when your hand can get caught up close to the body in a way that makes it difficult to access effective targets. This may be a good alternative. Grab onto the love handles with one or both hands, squeeze and twist the skin sharply. Gradual pressure is not as effective as it gives the attacker time to mentally steel himself to the pain *(Figure 4.32)*.

F4.32

Kidneys

A strong, penetrating blow to the kidneys can be quite painful, similar to what it feels like to be hit in the groin. It usually causes a person to arch back into the strike. Bear in mind that most of the effectiveness of this target comes from pain, but there are other bodily reactions that might still give a pain resistant attacker a moment's pause.

Method of Attack

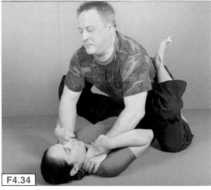

Heel kicks. This is the most likely way you'll target the kidneys for self-protection. If the attacker is between your legs, lift legs up and hook your heels to perform penetrating kicks to the kidneys *(Figure 4.33–4.34)*.

Legs and Arms

Knees and Shins

The knees and shins make for good targets when you are on the ground while your attacker is standing. A strike to these areas can be quite painful and can even cause a person to lose their balance and/or footing depending on your timing. A strong blow to the knee, particularly the knee cap, can cause damage that can incapacitate the leg (either temporarily or over the long term). Bear in mind that if your attacker is pain-resistant, using kicks to these areas to make them lose their balance and/or footing will be more beneficial for self-protection.

Methods of Attack

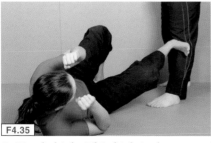

1. Turtle kick. This kick is the most effective choice when your attacker is in front of you and you are on your back. Turn your toes out to maximize your striking surface, and emphasize striking with your heel for power.
2. Side kick. Use this kick when your attacker comes in near your legs while you are on your side. Curl your toes back, keeping your heel higher. Emphasize the strike from your heel for power.

Inner Thighs and Arms

The skin of the inner thighs, close to the groin, and inner arms, close to the armpits, is more sensitive than other areas because it is so unexposed. When attacked, it can be quite painful. If your attacker is pain-resistant, however, they may be able to easily shrug it off, if they notice it at all. Use this target appropriately.

Methods of Attack

1. Pinch. Sometimes the groin is just out of reach, but you may have enough reach to do a pinch. For an effective pinch, grasp the skin between your thumb and the inside of your index knuckle: pinch, twist and pull. This can also be used on the inner arms *(Figure 4.37)*.

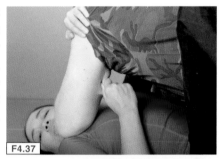

F4.37

F4.38

F4.39

2. Horse bite. Sometimes it is easier to access the inner thigh from the back. In this case, a horse bite is usually more effective. A horse bite may also be used to help move or control your attacker's arm. To do this type of pinch, reinforce your fingers together then clamp down on the skin sharply, digging your nails into the flesh *(Figure 4.38–4.39)*.

3. Bite. If your head is caught up in someone's arm or legs and you're struggling to find a good target, a sharp bite into the attacker's inner thigh or arm can be effective. Bite down sharply then shake your head from side to side while growling loudly. You're going for the effect of tearing skin. The psychological effect of this highly effective *(Figure 4.40)*.

F4.40

Fingers and Toes

The fingers and toes have a greater number and higher distribution of pain sensors than other joints in the body. As a result, the pain that is caused by attacks to the digits can still penetrate through to a person whose senses are mildly dulled, making them appropriate targets against a some pain-resistant attackers. If you manage to break a finger, this will effectively take your attackers hand out of the fight, helping to give you an advantage. Fingers are, of course, a more likely target, but toes can have their place too if your attacker isn't wearing shoes.

Methods of Attack

F4.41

F4.42

1. Bending back. Bending fingers back sharply can be a good way to break a solid grip. The toes can be bent back in a similar way if your attacker is controlling you with their legs from the rear *(Figure 4.41–4.42)*.
2. Splitting the fingers. If you manage to get a hold on an attacker's hand with both your hands, you can take out more fingers if you grab them and split them out to the sides *(Figure 4.43)*.

F4.43

Lateral and Anterior Femoral

These are regions on the outside and inside of the thighs that contain many nerve endings that are close to the surface of the leg. A solid blow to either area can cause pain (also known as a "Charlie horse") and motor dysfunction to the leg. Pressure with a boney surface can sometimes even be enough to cause pain. While the pain may not matter much to a pain-resistant attacker, a motor dysfunction may make it harder for your attacker to use their leg effectively, whether it's on the ground or when they attempt to run after you once you're on your feet.

Methods of Attack

1. Elbow strike to lateral femoral. If your attacker is using a form of side control to hold you down and your arms are up, you may be able to strike the lateral femoral with an elbow. You may also do this as an additional strike as you control your attacker's legs as you get to your feet. Use the tip of the elbow for maximum penetration *(Figure 4.44)*.

2. Elbow pressure to anterior femoral. This attack may be an option if you're caught up within your attacker's legs. Drive the tip of your elbow into the anterior femoral as sharply as possible so the attacker doesn't have time to mentally prepare for the pain *(Figure 4.45)*.

Wrists

When an attacker has your wrists pinned to the ground, you may find that you have very few options for targets. The wrists are quite boney, with little flesh providing a protective cushion. If your attacker's wrists are close enough to your head, you can resort to biting to help free your arm.

Method of Attack

Biting the wrist. Bite down sharply into your attacker's wrist using your incisors while making a growling sound for psychological impact *(Figure 4.46)*.

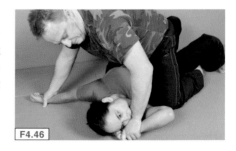

Using Weapons of Opportunity

Professor Georges Sylvain, founder of Can-ryu Jiu-jitsu, explained the concept of "weapons of opportunity" through the use of analogy. It seems appropriate to let his words introduce this section:

A weapon of opportunity is an object that lies conveniently at hand at the moment of an attack, and is used as an improvised weapon in defense. For example, let's assume you went to the grocery store and bought a can of beans. The clerk places it in a plastic bag for you to carry home. While you're carrying it to the front door of your home, you're suddenly pounced upon by an assailant. Reflexively, you swing the bag with the can of beans back at him, hitting his head. The can of beans has now become a weapon of opportunity. You didn't buy it with the purpose of walking around the city and hitting people over the head with it. You used it because that's what you happened to have in your hands to defend yourself with when you were subjected to an unprovoked physical assault.

Back when I lived in Ottawa, I read about a teenaged girl who was attacked while inline skating in the park. She was knocked down on her back but as the attacker moved in to get on top of her she kicked him in the groin with her skate and giving her the opportunity to escape. In another incident I read about a few years ago, a 50-year-old woman was attacked by a sex offender on the beach. He pushed her to the ground and forced himself on top of her. She successfully repelled the attack, however, by screaming and throwing sand in his face. These weren't people who had any particular training. They just used what they had at hand to mount a defense.

Whether you have training or not, weapons of opportunity can be used to enhance your self-protection strategy by reinforcing your attacks to vital targets or hindering your assailant's efforts to attack you. Furthermore, because improvised weapons are often overlooked as a threat, they can have an additional element of surprise that can make them even more effective. That being said, if you choose to use an improvised weapon, be sure that using it will actually support your goal of self-protection. If it doesn't, it is, at best, a distraction and, at worst, a waste of time and precious energy.

Improvised Hand Weapons

Improvised hand weapons can be useful for making strikes and other attacks to vulnerable targets more effective. There are a variety of sources for improvised weapons. They can be things you carry with you on your person, like a pen or a hand umbrella. They can also be things from your environment, like a rock from the ground or a bottle in a restaurant.

The ways they can be used vary depending on the type of weapon you have in hand. A pen or a small flashlight, or something similar, can be used

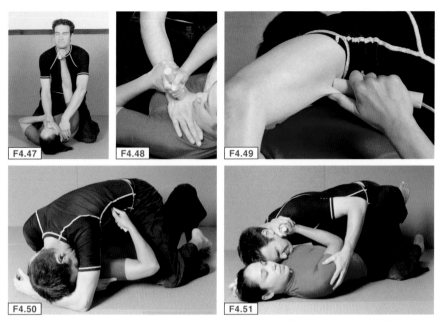

in a fist load grip to strike or cause pain an attacker. Because of the shape of these items, you can use either side to strike, or you might use the ends to apply pressure to vital targets *(Figure 4.47–4.51)*.

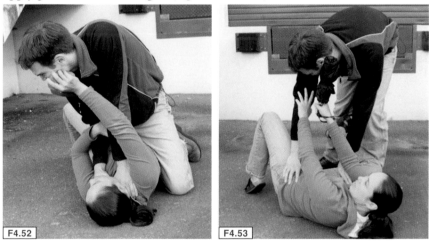

A rock, brick, or similarly sized and shaped items can be used in a palm load grip to strike an attacker. In certain situations, you might find them effective as a projectile weapon. For example, you might be able to throw a rock at a person as they approach you on the ground to give yourself enough time to get up to your feet. A baton-like item, like a bottle, hand umbrella or stick, may give you extra reach and can be used to swing at your attacker *(Figure 4.52–4.53)*.

Impairing Vision

Certain types of improvised weapons may be useless as hand weapons, but can be used to attack their eyes, impairing vision and causing pain. Sand or gravel may be thrown in an attacker's eyes. Certain liquids, like hairspray or cleaning products, can be painful when rubbed into eyes *(Figure 4.54–4.55)*.

F4.54

Stationary Objects

Stationary objects, like a wall or car, may be used to enhance your ground defense as well. If there is a wall behind you, bridging your attacker may cause them to smash their head into it. As you get to your feet, you may also use certain types of stationary objects to keep a barrier between you and your attacker *(Figure 4.56)*.

F4.55

F4.56

This chapter only scratches the surface of the various kinds of weapons of opportunity available. Each situation is different and presents different types of improvised weapons. By being aware and adaptive, you are better able to take advantage of the variety of tools available to you in your individual situation. Bear in mind that while using weapons of opportunity can increase the level of force in a way that serves you in your defense, you may need to be justify that increase in force legally.

CHAPTER 5

How to Breakfall on Concrete

Breakfalls are taught at many martial arts schools to allow students to be thrown safely for training purposes. Generally speaking, they are performed in a controlled environment with mats to minimize the risk of injury. That being said, even though their primary purpose is for safe training, you do learn air sense and body movements that help prevent injury from falls, whether it's in a defensive situation or a day-to-day life scenario like slipping on ice.

I have personally fallen on pavement a number of times without taking serious injury. I once did a full end-over on my bike suffering only a minor bruise where my saddle hit my thigh. I was able to do this by controlling the bike handlebars with my hands and absorbing the majority of the shock with my feet and upper back. Another time I saved myself when I skidded out on some gravel while riding my scooter. I managed to do a front roll, pop back to my feet, and even managed to catch my scooter so it didn't take too much damage, completely baffling the group I was riding with at the time. I've heard countless accounts from my own students and fellow jiu-jitsu practitioners who fell on hard surfaces and crediting breakfalls for their lack of injury.

The truth is that we're far more likely to suffer a fall in our day-to-day lives than we are to need to protect ourselves against a human attacker. For this reason alone, it is worthwhile to work breakfalls into your regular training regimen. In this chapter, you'll learn how to do a few basic breakfalls on mats for training purposes, as well as how they can be adapted should you have to use them on a hard surface. Please note that it is not recommended to practice breakfalls on hard surfaces. The techniques for taking a fall on a hard surface can and should be practiced on mats.

Even when training on mats, you first learn to do breakfalls under controlled circumstances, first on your own without being thrown. A training partner working with someone who is new to breakfalls should stick to simple takedowns, going only to position then letting the person lower themselves down at whatever pace they are comfortable with. As you build your confidence in your breakfall skills gradually, you'll be able to take falls at a higher speed and intensity.

How Breakfalls Work

Breakfalls are one of the most unnatural things we learn to do in Can-ryu Jiu-jitsu. Our brains aren't usually hardwired to perform breakfalls. Our instinctive reactions to falls are to try and use our hands and arms to catch ourselves, putting us at risk of a variety of injuries to wrists, shoulders, collar bones, etc. Nonetheless, they are important to learn so you keep yourself safe when training throws and takedowns regularly.

Breakfalls serve to protect against injury by distributing the impact over a greater surface area of your body so that no one part bears the full brunt of the fall. It's like lying on a bed of nails. If you're evenly distributed, no one part of your body gets punctured. When hitting the ground, it's important to stay relaxed. Stiffness causes the body to land unevenly, increasing your chance of injury. To help you relax, be sure to breathe out as you fall and hit the ground, like you're sighing. This also helps prevent from being winded on impact.

Backward Breakfall

This breakfall serves to protect you when you get taken down straight back toward the rear.

1. Take one step backward with either leg, looking over your shoulder. Transfer your weight onto the back leg, and lower yourself to the ground *(Figure 5.1–5.2)*.

2. Roll backward, slapping ground with the full length of both arms, from shoulder to fingertips *(Figure 5.3–5.4)*.

*Note: As you become more comfortable with this fall, you should try practicing it so that your tailbone doesn't touch down as you fall.

3. If an attacker is in close pursuit, you may kick them from here *(Figure 5.5)*.

F5.5

F5.7

4. If you have a little more time, you may roll up to one foot, deliver a kick, then immediately come back to your feet *(Figure 5.6–5.7)*.

F5.6

Backward Breakfall Over an Obstacle

Similar to the basic back breakfall, this one is used to simulate how it would feel to fall when tripping over something.

F5.8

F5.9

F5.10

1. Have a partner go on his hands and knees to create an obstacle on the ground. If you're just starting out, your partner can take a "stone" position so you can practice falling from a lower height *(Figure 5.8–5.10)*.

2. Back into your partner and place your hands on their back. Slide your hips over and just past their back.

3. Let go of your hands and allow yourself to fall to the ground, hitting with both arms and your upper back *(Figure 5.11)*. When starting

F5.11

out, you can slow yourself down by squeezing your partner's body with your calves to create a little drag. You'll likely start out leading with your hips and tailbone first, which doesn't really hurt when landing on mats. As you get more comfortable, you should try to avoid this to prevent potential tailbone injuries that could occur if falling on a hard surface. Do this by arching your back as you fall, so that you land on your upper back.

Side Breakfall—Static

Many types of throws or takedowns lead to a side fall of some sort. This type of breakfall is generally preferable to back breakfalls because there is less chance of hitting your spine or head.

1. Bend your left leg and draw your right arm and leg across your body.
2. Keep bending your left leg until your upper body is close to the ground.

3. Let your weight fall, hitting the ground with most of your body in one bang. Ideally, you'll hit the ground with the entire right side of your body, including most of your right leg and the full length of your right arm, shoulder to finger tips *(Figure 5.14)*. Your right leg should be fully straight to protect against knee impacts. Your left leg should be bent, knee pointing up, supported by the ball of your foot. Ensure that you are fully on your side and not on your back *(Figure 5.15)*.

4. Bring your right hand up to protect your face. Note that the left arm is bent with the elbow tucked to protect the ribs.

5. If your attacker is in close pursuit, you may deliver a side kick with your left leg *(Figure 5.16)*. To get up, support your weight with your right hand and draw your right leg through to the back so you can get up in a solid stance. Repeat on opposite side.

Side Breakfall—Traveling

This version of the side breakfall can be used when falling to the ground when pushed from the side.

1. Step your left leg behind and across your right leg. It should be a deep step *(Figure 5.17)*.
2. Bend your left leg until your upper body is close to the ground *(Figure 5.18)*.

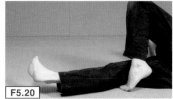

3. Let your weight fall, hitting the ground with most of your body at once. Ideally, you'll hit the ground with the entire right side of your body, including most of your right leg and the full length of your right arm, shoulder to finger tips. Your right leg should be straight to protect against knee impacts. Your left leg should be bent, knee pointing up, supported by the ball of your foot. Follow up with the same kicks and get up procedure as described for a static side breakfall. Repeat on opposite side *(Figure 5.19–5.20)*.

Forward Roll

This maneuver can be a great option for reducing impact when falling forward.

1. With your right leg forward, lean forward with your right arm extended, pinkie finger up, and your left hand supporting your weight *(Figure 5.21)*.
2. Springing off your right foot, rotate your body over your left hand, rolling down your right arm to the shoulder then diagonally across your back. You should keep your right arm stiff, with a slight bend at the elbow *(Figure 5.22)*. Do not let it collapse or tuck it under your body while rolling.

3. While rolling, bend your left leg and tuck it under your body *(Figure 5.23)*.
4. As you come to your feet, turn in your stance and be prepared to kick if your attacker is in pursuit *(Figure 5.24)*. Repeat on the opposite side.

Forward Breakfall

If a roll is not possible, either because your legs are caught up in something or there is not space to roll, this breakfall can be used to reduce impact and the potential for injury.

1. Bend your knees to a squat position *(Figure 5.25)*.
2. Spring from your knees and shoot your legs back, while levelling your upper body in the air *(Figure 5.26)*.

3. Hit the ground using both arms from elbow to fingertips. Your arms should form a diamond framing your head. Your lower body is supported by the balls of your feet separated to be a little wider than shoulder width apart. Be sure to turn your face before you hit the ground so that you don't hit face first if you mess up your breakfall *(Figure 5.27)*.
4. Turn on to your side and be ready to kick back if your attacker is in pursuit then get to your feet *(Figure 5.28)*.

Breakfalls on Mats vs. Breakfalls on Hard Surfaces

F5.29

F5.30

F5.31

F5.32

When performing breakfalls on hard surfaces, like floors or pavement, the fundamentals described at the beginning of the chapter still apply. But when it's a hard surface, it is that much more important to absorb the impact over a greater surface area of your body, to stay relaxed and to breathe out as you fall.

The only difference is that, unless you happen to have protective gloves on, you don't want to engage your hands in the breakfalls. Your skin of your hands could get torn, plus your hands have much smaller bones, which are more likely to get injured on a hard surface. To do this, you need to engage your forearm muscles and bend your hand back at the wrist.

Doing breakfalls on concrete is still far from ideal. Even with good form, there is still a good chance of getting minor cuts and bruises, but if you do breakfalls with proper technique, you're a lot less likely to receive major injuries like broken bones or joint sprains.

CHAPTER 6

Defending From the Ground Against a Standing Attacker

In the last chapter, you learned how to do breakfalls to minimize the potential injury should you be taken to the ground by an attacker. Once you're on the ground though, you want to get back to your feet as quickly as possible to avoid the dangers of fighting from the ground as described in Chapter 1. Before you have the chance to get back to your feet though, you may have to deal with attacks from the still-standing attacker. This chapter teaches you to deal with such attacks and give yourself the opportunity to get back to your feet.

The Nature of the Attack

If you've been taken to the ground, whether you've been knocked down from a strike or have fallen to the ground in some other way in the course of an attack, your attacker may choose to deal with you from a standing position rather than follow you down. Very commonly this ends up being a kick to the head. This type of attack can be extremely dangerous to you if it lands, with the potential to cause spinal injuries, brain damage, even death. It is therefore vital to protect against this type of attack.

Alternatively, your attacker may try to press his advantage by trying to get on top of you. If they decide to do this, they usually try to come around your legs instinctively knowing that your legs pose the greatest threat.

Ultimately, your first goal is to get back to your feet. So if your attacker doesn't immediately press the advantage, you should attempt to get back to your feet as soon as you're able to do so safely. Many people will be distracted by their "victory" if they land what they think is a knock-out blow, even if all they do is knock you down. Take advantage by getting to your feet as quickly as possible and escaping if you have the opportunity.

Body Shifting Principles to Keep in Mind

Keeping your legs between you and your attacker is the primary body shifting principle you would use against a standing attacker when you're on the ground. This keeps your head safer by keeping it at the farthest distance from your attacker. In addition, your legs can be used to kick your attacker as he closes in on you. Alternatively, you can use your knees to keep your attacker at a safer distance if he closes in on you too quickly for you to get in an effective kick. Either way, it is important to keep your legs between you and your attacker.

Vital Targets to Attack

When you're on the ground and your attacker is standing, the most important areas you can attack are ones that are accessible using your legs. This includes the shins, knees and groin. The power that can be generated from kicks, even from the ground, can result in painful blows to the shins or knees. When targeting the shin, you may also disrupt your attacker's balance, particularly if they are mid-step, causing them to stumble or fall. When targeting knees, there is good chance of causing serious injury to the joint, which can make it difficult or impossible for the attacker to pursue you once you get to your feet. A kick to the groin, on the other hand, may not be possible when the attacker is at a distance depending on the length of your legs, but it can be a great debilitating target if they close in on you.

When attempting to get back up to your feet, it's a good idea to follow up with some sort of strike to keep your attacker from coming after you if you believe they are still a threat. Hand strikes to the groin or elbow strikes to the lateral femoral are good options for this.

Defense: Kicking from the Ground

1. If your attacker is approaching you from straight in front of your legs, stay flat on your back with both legs bent. This makes it harder for your attacker to judge your distance but also makes it easier for you to move and kick *(Figure 6.1)*.

2. If they get in range of your legs, kick at their shin or knee using a turtle kick, emphasizing the heel with the toes turned out for maximum striking surface *(Figure 6.2)*.

3. If they try to come around your legs turn on to your side and move with them using the body shifting shown in Chapter 3, keeping your legs bent. This makes it harder for your attacker to judge your distance but also makes it easier for you to move and kick *(Figure 6.3)*.

4. If the attacker gets within your kicking range, kick at their shin or knee using a side kick. If you're a law enforcement officer and are carrying tools on your side, you should try to maneuver with your back down as your tools will likely impede your movement *(Figure 6.4)*.

5. If the attacker gets around your legs and starts to lower himself in order to mount you, push off their leg, lifting your legs around theirs (See Chapter

F6.7   F6.8

3 for a more detailed description). Follow up with straight heel kicks to the groin or solar plexus if your legs are too long to target the groin *(Figure 6.5–6.8)*.

*Tip: A good way to train this at speed without risk of injury to your partner is to use a body shield. When holding the shield, move around the defender as though trying to get around their legs. Every so often, extend the shield out into their kicking range to give them a target to kick. Make sure you don't hold it against your legs as the force can extend through the target and can potentially cause injury to your knee.

Defense: Mount Attempt—Late

If your attacker manages to step over your body before you have the chance to push off their leg, you have one more opportunity to defend before they lower their weight.

1. Grab the back of your attacker's feet with both hands and deliver a heel kick to the groin *(Figure 6.9)*.

2. Follow through with your kick to push the attacker back to make them fall backward, tripping against your hands *(Figure 6.10)*.

F6.9   F6.10

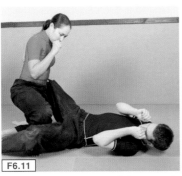

3. Keeping control of the attacker's legs with one arm and your knee, deliver an open hand strike to the groin *(Figure 6.11)*.

4. Spread the knees open from the inside to keep the attacker from kicking you as you get back on your feet *(Figure 6.12)*.

Variation

If you have long legs or simply aren't able to get your foot up in time, you can use the knee as shown in this variation.

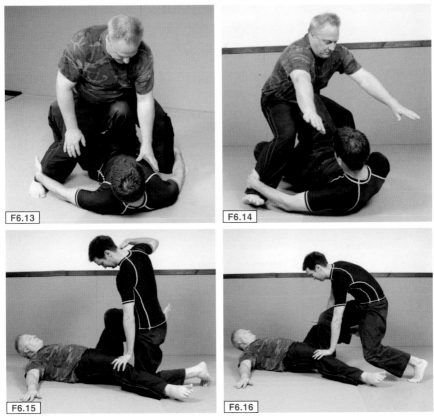

1. Grab the back of your attacker's feet with both hands and drive your knee up into their groin as they lower down *(Figure 6.13)*.

2. Follow through with your knee to push the attacker back to make them fall backward, tripping against your hands *(Figure 6.14)*. Keeping control of the attacker's legs with one arm and your knee, deliver an open hand strike to the groin *(Figure 6.15)*.

3. Spread the knees open from the inside to keep the attacker from kicking you as you get back on your feet *(Figure 6.16)*.

Defense: Kick to Head

1. As your attacker comes around your legs, winding up to kick your head, your hands should be up and ready to block the kick with a double fore-

arm block. If possible, use the meatiest part of your forearm to take the kick as this will provide the most amount of surface area with which to absorb the shock *(Figure 6.17–6.20)*. As the kick makes contact your arms should be firm but spring-like so that they can absorb the energy of the kick. If you're stiff and tense, you'll feel greater shock to your arms and will be more likely to experience injury. You will likely have to block more than one kick like this so be prepared for repeated kicks. Make sure your arms provide enough resistance to absorb the force of the kick otherwise the attacker may just kick right through your block *(Figure 6.21)*.

Do not reach out for the kick as this reducing the surface area with which you can block, making it easier for them to come around your arms and kick your head *(Figure 6.22–6.23)*.

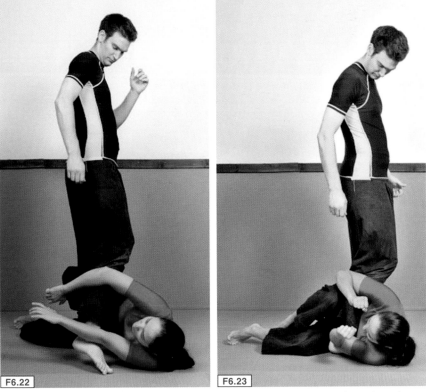

F6.22   F6.23

2. At the earliest opportunity, wrap your arms around the kicking leg, drawing your legs around their other leg. Your body encircles the feet drawing them together to take away the attacker's base. See variation on the next page if you can't reach the other leg with your legs.
3. If done quickly, the attacker will likely lose their balance forward or backward. Whichever way they go, roll in that direction to force them down to the ground *(Figure 6.24–6.25)*.

4. Keep control of your attacker's legs as you come to your knees. Deliver an elbow strike to the lateral femoral area, if appropriate *(Figure 6.27)*.
5. Push into the attacker's legs to keep them under control as you come to your feet *(Figure 6.28)*.

Variation

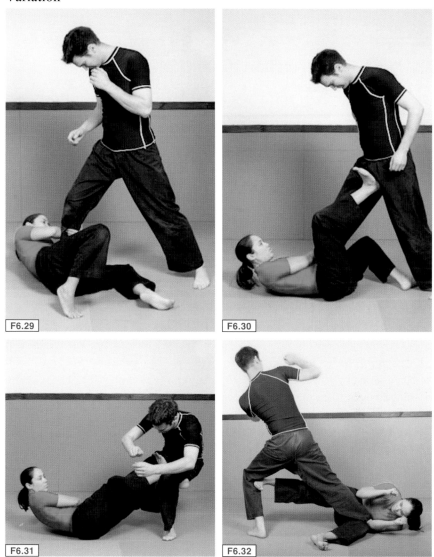

F6.29

F6.30

F6.31

F6.32

1. If you can't reach the other leg with your legs, draw them around the kick-ing leg *(Figure 6.29)*.
2. While keeping control of the kicking leg with one leg and your arms, deliver a heel kick to the groin with your opposite leg. Alternatively, you can deliver a side kick to their opposite knee *(Figure 6.30–6.32)*. Keep kick-ing until your attacker is sufficiently incapacitated for you to get to your feet safely.

CHAPTER 7

Defending Against a Mounted Attacker

In the last chapter, you learned to deal with a standing attacker when you're prone on the ground. If the attacker gets past your legs, you're vulnerable to being mounted. It is, of course, safer for you as a defender to keep this from happening using the techniques you saw in the previous chapter. But if you fail to keep the attacker from getting around or controlling your legs, it is important to know how to handle a variety of attacks from the mounted position.

The Nature of the Attack

When an attacker is mounted on top of your body, he is in a dominant position with gravity on his side. This can be quite intimidating, particularly if the attacker is bigger and stronger. From this position, the attacker can attack you in a number of ways. He can attempt a choke, punch your head, or if he is skilled enough, he could also attack the joints in the arm, like the elbow and shoulder. Alternatively, he could simply aim to tire you out and/or hold you down while waiting for "help" from his friends.

The attacker's weight is, however, largely localized in one spot: under their hips, which leaves opportunities for defense. If the attacker is not an experienced ground fighter, it can be relatively easy to off-balance him and create openings for escape using a combination of body shifting and attacks to vital targets, even when there is a size advantage. However, if the attacker has some understanding of weight transfer principles, it can make your job a lot tougher, even more so when there is a size advantage.

No matter what type of attacker you're facing, it is important for you to maintain a strong will and to keep fear from overwhelming your will to fight back.

Body Shifting Principles to Keep in Mind

Bridging and rolling is one of the primary body shifting principles that can be used against a mounted attacker. If the attacker has placed his weight over your hips, then you can use the hip thrust from bridging to take the weight off your body. You can then follow through with a body roll to reverse the attacker onto his back.

In some cases shrimping may also be necessary. If the attacker has his weight placed on your chest, you can use shrimping to put the attacker's weight back over his hips so that bridging and rolling can be used. Bridging and rolling may still prove difficult, even with the attacker's weight on the defender's hips, especially if the attacker is much heavier. In some cases, shrimping may be an easier way for a much smaller defender to displace the attacker's weight and create space to escape.

If the attacker has ground fighting experience, you will likely need to use a combination of bridging and rolling, as well as shrimping.

Vital Targets to Attack

When being mounted, there are two important areas you can attack when your hands are free; the head and the groin. Since it is difficult for the attacker to defend both his head and groin areas simultaneously, this makes it easier to disrupt the attack.

Vulnerable targets on the head include: eyes, nose, chin/jaw, throat and ears. Depending on how the attacker is holding his head, you may be able to rake your fingers across the eyes, deliver a palm strike to the nose or chin/jaw, deliver a v-hand strike to the throat or attack the ears by slapping them or ripping them. If your hands are being held down, preventing their use, you may use a bite to the attacker's wrist to free one hand to facilitate other strikes.

Vulnerable targets in the groin area include the testicles and inner thigh. You can slide your hand under the testicles to grab and squeeze them. If you're having trouble accessing the underside of the groin, you can alternatively pinch and twist the sensitive skin of the upper inner thigh.

It is important to realize that no one target will necessarily be accessible in every mounted attack. To increase your chances of escape, you should be prepared to look for whatever target opportunities are available as the attack changes. If the attacker blocks the groin, you should immediately switch to one of the head targets like the eyes, for example. If the attacker then blocks the eyes, you should go back for the groin. When the attacker is put on the defense, you should then make use of body shifting to create an opportunity for escape.

Defense: Two Hands on Throat

1. Drop your chin and raise your shoulders to minimize the effectiveness of the choke. Strike a vulnerable target, or multiple targets, to distract the attacker and/or weaken their grip *(Figure 7.1–7.2)*.
2. Pin one leg with your foot while wrapping your arms around your attacker's elbow, hugging it strongly to your hip. If you are pinning your attacker's right foot, your arms should wrap their right arm *(Figure 7.3–7.5)*.

3. Bridge your hips up explosively, rolling toward the pinned leg and arm of the attacker. By keeping the foot pinned, you prevent your attacker from sprawling with their leg to stop the roll over *(Figure 7.6)*.

4. If the attacker frees their arm and posts it to prevent the roll, re-establish control over the arm and re-attempt the roll over *(Figure 7.7–7.8)*.

5. Roll up onto your knees keeping control of one of the legs. Deliver a finger whip strike to the testicles to prevent the attacker from continuing further aggressive actions *(Figure 7.9)*.

6. Spread the knees open from the inside to keep the attacker from kicking you as you get back on your feet. If the attacker blocks your attempt to bridge and roll, and successfully re-establishes a mounted position, be prepared to return to the use of attacks to vital targets to regain opportunities to

bridge and roll. Switching the side you pin can help surprise your attacker. You may also attempt to use the shrimping maneuver described in steps 3-4 of "Defense: Postured Up Position" on page 90 , which can also work if your attacker manages to sprawl with his leg.

Defense: One Hand on Each Wrist (Weight on Body)

This position can be a very difficult one from which to escape, especially if the attacker has a significant size advantage. That being said, it is less dangerous for you in the sense that there is no immediate physical danger, unless there are multiple attackers involved. If you're smaller, it may be more practical for you to wait until the attacker does something different to more easily mount a defense using less energy. This could be when the attacker changes his attack, goes to undo his pants, or reaches for a weapon. That being said, there may be an urgent reason why you might want to try to escape immediately.

1. Use shrimping to offset the attacker's weight from your wrists, gradually drawing them up onto your chest *(Figure 7.11)*. If the attacker is too strong or heavy, try to distract him first by biting into one of his wrists.

  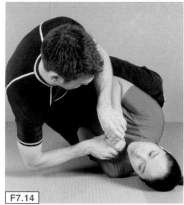

2. Pin one leg with your foot and bridge your hips up explosively, rolling toward the pinned leg of the attacker. By keeping the foot pinned, you prevent your attacker from sprawling with their leg *(Figure 7.12–7.14)*.

3. If the attacker lets go of your wrist to post their arm and prevent the roll, establish control over the arm by hugging it strongly to your hip then re-attempt the roll-over *(Figure 7.15–7.16)*.

4. Roll up onto your knees, keeping control of one of the legs. Deliver a finger whip strike to the testicles to prevent the attacker from continuing any aggressive actions.

5. Spread the knees open from the inside to keep the attacker from kicking you as you get back to your feet *(Figure 7.17)*.

If the attacker blocks your attempt to bridge and roll, and successfully re-establishes a mounted position, be prepared to return to the use of attacks to vital targets to regain opportunities to bridge and roll. Switching the side you pin can help surprise your attacker. You may also attempt to use the shrimping maneuver described in steps 3 and 4 of "Defense: Postured Up

Position" on page 90, which also works if your attacker manages to sprawl with his leg.

Defense: One Hand on Each Wrist (Weight on Wrists)

In some cases in this position, your attacker might be more focused on pinning your wrists rather than keeping your body controlled. In this case, you are likely to need a different approach than the one described above. Try this one instead.

1. All in one motion, bridge your hips up explosively while driving your wrist toward your legs sharply, angling your wrists toward your attacker's thighs *(Figure 7.18–7.20)*.

2. Do a horse bite pinch to your attacker's inner thigh with one hand while pinning their foot on the same side with your foot *(Figure 7.21)*.
3. As their hips lift, reacting from the pain of the pinch, drive the middle knuckle of your opposite hand into their ribs, while you bridge your hips and roll into the strike *(Figure 7.22–7.23)*.

F7.24   F7.25

4. Roll up onto your knees, keeping control of the legs. Deliver a finger whip strike to the testicles to prevent the attacker from continuing any aggressive actions *(Figure 7.24)*.
5. Spread the knees open from the inside to keep the attacker from kicking you as you get back to your feet *(Figure 7.25)*.

Defense: Ground and Pound

Being punched in the head is always a risk when mounted. If your attacker is not attempting to hold you down or control your arms in any way, you should keep them up in a guard to protect your head. Expect to get hit, but keep your wits about you to minimize the damage and look for the best opportunities to fight back.

F7.26   F7.27

1. Keep your arms up and close to your head while keeping your chin tucked down and your shoulders raised. This makes your most vulnerable targets (i.e. nose, chin/jaw, temples) harder to strike. Keep your eyes open and be prepared to move your head to minimize the effectiveness of the blows as much as possible *(Figure 7.26–7.27)*.

F7.28

F7.29

2. While the attacker is punching, they commit some of their body weight forward to make their strikes more powerful. Wrap one of their arms around the elbow as they punch, hugging it strongly into your hip while pinning his foot on the same side with your own foot *(Figure 7.28–7.29)*.

F7.30

F7.31

F7.32

F7.33

3. Bridge your hips up explosively, rolling toward the pinned leg and arm of the attacker. By keeping the foot pinned, you prevent your attacker from sprawling with his leg. The attacker is likely to punch as you roll, so be sure to keep the shoulder on your exposed side raised and chin tucked to

minimize the effectiveness of any strikes. If the attacker posts their arm to prevent the roll, re-establish control over the arm and re-attempt the roll-over *(Figure 7.30–7.32)*.

4. Roll up onto your knees keeping control of one of the legs. Deliver a finger whip to the testicles to prevent the attacker from continuing any aggressive actions.

5. Spread the knees open from the inside to keep the attacker from kicking you as you get back on your feet *(Figure 7.33)*.

   If the attacker blocks your attempt to bridge and roll, and successfully re-establishes a mounted position, be prepared to return to the use of attacks to vital targets to regain opportunities to bridge and roll. Switching the side you pin can serve to surprise your attacker. You may also attempt to use the shrimping maneuver described in steps 3-4 of "Defense: Postured Up Position" on below, which also works if your attacker manages to sprawl with his leg.

Defense: Postured Up Position

An attacker may decide to simply maintain his position in mount, either to hold you down while he waits for his friends to come help, to give him an opportunity to access a weapon or to simply tire you out to make it easier to attack or control you. Be prepared to defend against other types of attack from this position in case your attacker decides to change his approach.

  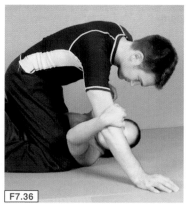

F7.34   F7.35   F7.36

1. If the attacker is sitting high on your chest, use shrimping to push their weight down to your hips. If the attacker is particularly heavy, you may facilitate this by attacking the testicles or if inaccessible, pinching the inner thigh *(Figure 7.34–7.35)*.

2. With your attacker's hips now over your hips, pin one foot with your own foot and bridge your hips up, in an attempt to force him to post. If he posts his arm, follow steps 2 to 5 from "Defense: One Hand on Each Wrist" on page 86.

3. If the attacker maintains his base without posting his arm, either by remaining upright, catching his weight with his foot or by sprawling, attempt to shrimp out from under his base. This method can also be used in any of the other positions if you fail to keep the leg pinned with your foot when bridging and rolling *(Figure 7.37–7.39)*.

4. Use this opportunity to free your legs and kick up toward the head, solar plexus or ribs, whatever target is most accessible, getting to your feet as soon as possible *(Figure 7.40–7.41)*.

If the attacker is skilled or has a significant size advantage, it may take several attempts at shrimping and/or bridging and rolling to escape. If you find opportunities to attack vital targets, use them to help facilitate your body shifting, or vice versa, use body shifting to facilitate your attacks to vital targets.

CHAPTER 8

Defending Against an
Attacker From Guard

In the last chapter, you learned to deal with an attacker from the disadvantageous position of the underside of a mount. If you manage to keep your legs between you and your attacker though, you may end up in a position in which the attacker is between your legs, a position commonly known as the "guard" position. This is also a position from which rape may be attempted. While not as safe as dealing with an attacker from your feet, it is certainly safer than being on the underside of a mount or side controlling position as you are able to use your legs for control or to kick at your attacker so you can get quickly back to your feet.

The Nature of the Attack

When you are being attacked from between your legs, you aren't at much of a disadvantage except for the fact that you're on the ground. In grappling sports like BJJ, the guard is considered an advantageous position opening up a wide variety of submissions and sweeps.

Some of these maneuvers, particularly sweeps, can be useful for reversing your position in a street defense situation if you're skilled at applying them. That being said, they may not be as easy to apply when being attacked by a much bigger, heavier attacker and/or one who is not following any rule system, striking at any and every available target. They can easily attack your groin from this position if you're not actively protecting it.

Attempting submissions, on the other hand, can be dangerous as the majority of ones that can be applied from this position are applied from your back, leaving you tied up and dangerously exposed to multiple attackers.

When you are at a size/strength disadvantage and have no reason to want to control the attacker, the safest option is to create an opportunity to get back to your feet as quickly as possible. From this position, it isn't as hard to do as it is from the underside of a mount or side controlling position as your attacker isn't as easily able to use their weight to control you. Furthermore, you can more easily use your legs to control their body or to kick at your attacker.

If you stay calm, keep yourself protected and look for and/or create opportunities to use your legs, you can find your way back to your feet without too much difficulty.

Body Shifting Principles to Keep in Mind

Shrimping is the primary body shifting principle that can be used against an attacker from guard. It can allow you to create the space necessary to use your legs to kick at your attacker's vital targets. That being said, shrimping on its own may not be enough to create sufficient space, particularly if you have long legs relative to your attacker's body size. In such cases, you'll likely need to supplement shrimping with strikes to open up even more space in order to use your legs.

Vital Targets to Attack

When in guard, you have a wide variety of options for vital targets to attack. Depending on your leg length relative to your attacker's body length, one option is to shrimp on to your side and kick the attacker's solar plexus or ribs. If you have the leg flexibility and your attacker doesn't have too much weight placed on your hips, you may also be able to use your heels to strike at your attacker's kidneys.

People with longer legs relative to their attacker's body length who aren't able to easily use their legs in this way will likely have arm reach to compensate. They are more likely to be able to strike at the head area with their hands effectively, targeting eyes, nose, ears or jaw. By targeting these areas they can cause the attacker to flinch or draw back which can create the necessary space for them to use their legs to then kick at the attacker.

If the attacker, however, drops their upper body weight into you rather than holding it back, other head targets become accessible. You can grab the attacker's hair, strike the back of their head, drive your thumb into their eye, scratch their face, rip their ear or apply pressure to the tip of the nose or the mandibular angle. These can all be used to manipulate the attacker's body weight to create opportunities to deliver more damaging strikes or reverse your position.

With all the options open from this position, you can be more resourceful in terms of summoning up the best defense for your body type, in whatever situation you find yourself.

Defense: Two Hands on Throat

1. Grip your attacker's wrists, while dropping your chin and raising your shoulders to minimize the effectiveness of the choke *(Figure 8.1)*.
2. Shrimp onto your side keeping control of the wrists *(Figure 8.2)*.

3. Deliver a turtle kick your attacker in the solar plexus or ribs, thrusting back to create more space *(Figure 8.3)*.
4. If they're still a threat and within range, deliver a heel kick toward their chin or nose *(Figure 8.4)*.
5. Get to your feet as soon as it is safe to do so *(Figure 8.5)*.

Defense: Two Hands on Throat (Long Legs)

Use this method if your legs are too long to get enough space between you and your attacker.

1. Grip your attacker's wrist with one hand, drop your chin and raise your shoulders to minimize the effectiveness of the choke *(Figure 8.6)*.
2. Using your free hand, attack your choice of vital target on the face. An open palm strike to the nose is demonstrated here *(Figure 8.7)*. The goal is to cause the attacker to take their weight off your neck.
3. Once the weight is off your neck, shrimp onto your side pushing off your attacker's leg to create distance *(Figure 8.8)*.

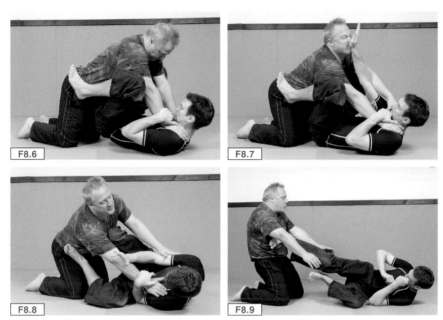

4. Deliver a side kick to your attacker's solar plexus, ribs or head, depending on which target is most easily accessible to you. Kick multiple times if necessary *(Figure 8.9)*.

5. Get to your feet as soon as it is safe to do so *(Figure 8.10–8.11)*.

Defense: One Hand on Each Wrist

1. Shrimp onto your side with your legs coiled *(Figure 8.12–8.13)*.

2. Deliver a turtle kick to your attacker's solar plexus or ribs, thrusting through to create space *(Figure 8.14)*.
3. If they are still a threat and within range, deliver a heel kick to their chin or nose *(Figure 8.15)*.
4. Get to your feet as soon as it is safe to do so.

Defense: One Hand on Each Wrist (Long Legs)

If you have long legs relative to your attacker's body length, you may find you don't have enough space to do an effective kick after shrimping. Use this method instead.

1. Shrimp onto your side with your legs coiled *(Figure 8.16)*.
2. Using the foot of your lower leg, push your attacker's hip back to create space *(Figure 8.17)*.

3. Once you have enough space, deliver a side kick into your attacker's solar plexus or ribs. Kick multiple times if necessary *(Figure 8.18–8.19)*.

4. Get to your feet as soon as it is safe to do so *(Figure 8.20–8.21)*.

Defense: Ground & Pound

1. Draw your knees together and push into your attacker's chest. Do this as quickly as possible as they begin their barrage of strikes. Support their weight keeping them out of striking range of your head *(Figure 8.22–8.23)*.

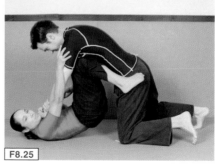

2. While your attacker is striking, they will likely commit more of their body weight forward to try and get closer to land their strikes. As they do so, let their weight collapse forward and to your side as you shrimp onto your side, preparing for a scissor sweep. Your lower leg is positioned to undercut your attacker's base at their knee or their foot if they're standing, close to the floor. Your upper leg's shin across the belly, hooking around their

body with your foot. If your attacker outweighs you by a wide margin, it may be preferable to use your knees to push the attacker back, creating space to kick at their vital targets with your legs *(Figure 8.24–8.25)*.

3. Follow this movement through scissoring your legs *(Figure 8.26–8.29)*.
4. Follow up with an open palm strike to the nose to distract your attacker to give yourself an opportunity to safely get to your feet. If your attacker is sufficiently immobilized that you can get to your feet safely, do so.
5. If your attacker continues to grab at you or struggle with you as you try to get up, drop your knee into their head and push off on it to get free.

*Warning: When striking from mount, you want to make sure that witnesses are aware that you are an unwilling participant in this fight. At the same time, you need to make sure you are able to immobilize your attacker sufficiently so that you have the opportunity to get out of the mount safely and escape. Be sure to vocalize as you strike, saying: "Let me go!" or "Stop it! I don't want to fight!" Don't let yourself get caught up in the heat of the moment. Only use as many strikes as is necessary to give your opportunity to escape. Depending on your situation, you could face charges of using excessive force.

CHAPTER 9

Defending Against an Attacker Mounted on Your Back

In the previous two chapters, you learned to deal with a person attacking you on the ground from in front of your body. While neither are a great position to be in from a defensive point of view, at least you're using forward loco-motion, which is more natural, when mounting a defense. In this chapter, you'll learn to deal with an attacker mounted on your back, one of the most dangerous positions to encounter while on the ground.

The Nature of the Attack

You are in an extremely compromised position in this situation. Obviously, you don't willingly adopt this position for any tactical advantages. If you end up in this position, it is probably after having been stunned, knocked out or overpowered.

This situation is particularly dangerous, not only because you have to fight gravity coupled with the weight of your attacker, but also because the body's structure and musculature is less effective when used for backward locomotion. Defensively, not only is it more difficult to use your arms to defend against blows or to strike out at an attacker's vital targets, it is also harder to see what attacks are coming, requiring you to feel the attacks or simply anticipate them. Body shifting techniques are also more difficult due to the use of backward locomotion.

Because you're so vulnerable in this situation, to have the best chances of escape, it is imperative to react quickly and aggressively to catch the attacker off guard.

Body Shifting Principles to Keep in Mind

Turtling is the only type of body shifting that can be used when defending against an attacker mounted on the back. You must use the ground for leverage using your elbows/forearms and knees to destabilize your attacker and gain a more favorable position from which to defend or to simply escape.

Vital Targets to Attack

There are fewer vital targets to attack from this position than from positions in which you're facing the attacker. There are some scenarios in which you could reach behind and grab the groin or pinch and twist sensitive areas such as the inner thigh or "love handles," but these targets may be out of reach or otherwise difficult to access and use effectively. Furthermore, you would still need to bring your arms back in front of you to use turtling to destabilize the attacker. Biting has the best chance of distracting an attacker if the arms are close enough to your mouth to be accessed. Because there are so few vital targets accessible from this position, you have the best chance of escape using body shifting to gain a more favorable position in which more effective options are available.

Defense: Two Hands on Neck

From this position it is harder for the attacker to get the hands around the victim's throat to cut off breathing unless the neck is very small and the attacker's hands are very large. That being said, there is a risk that the attacker could simply slam the victim's head against the ground.

F9.1   F9.2

1. Turtle up onto your forearms while dropping your chin and raising your shoulders to defend against strangulation. This position also makes it more difficult for the attacker to slam your head into the ground, while giving you a point of leverage to help destabilize the attacker *(Figure 9.1)*.

2. Bring one knee up over one of your attacker's legs to pin it down and prevent the attacker from sprawling *(Figure 9.2)*.

F9.3   F9.4

3. Push into the ground with your forearms, raising your hips to destabilize your attacker forward. Then turn in the direction of your attacker's pinned

leg to roll him over. A smaller person usually needs to turn more explosively, causing them to rotate all the way around as the roll over is performed. It is important not to pause when facing away from their attacker, and to keep control of his legs to prevent getting trapped in a rear guard. A larger, broader person may be able to simply shift the attacker's weight over without having to fully rotate their body *(Figure 9.3–9.4)*.

4. The attacker may let go of the neck and post their arm to prevent from being rolled. If they do, circle the arm with your arm and hold it tight while you re-attempt the roll-over *(Figure 9.5–9.6)*.

5. If you lose control of your attacker's leg, keep turning your body anyway. If you are slim, this will likely turn your position into a standard mount, which is an easier position from which to defend *(Figure 9.7)*.

6. As you come around after successfully rolling the attacker over, strike their groin with your elbow or your hand, whichever is more natural from the new position *(Figure 9.8)*.

7. Control the legs with your arms, spreading them out to prevent kick attacks as you get to your feet *(Figure 9.9)*.

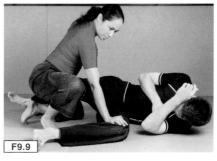

Defense: One Hand on Each Wrist

This position can be very difficult to escape, especially if you're much smaller than your attacker. It is, however, less dangerous for you in the sense that there is no immediate physical danger, unless there are multiple attackers involved. If you're smaller, it may be more practical to wait until the attacker does something different to more easily mount a defense that uses less energy. This could be when the attacker changes his attack, goes to undo his pants, or reaches for a weapon. That being said, there may be an urgent reason why you might want to try to escape immediately.

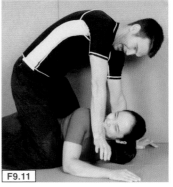

F9.10   F9.11

1. If the wrists are close enough to your head, attempt to bite one of the attacker's wrists to distract him *(Figure 9.10–9.11)*. Follow up by turtling up onto your forearms, bringing them as close together as possible, while shrugging your shoulders up in case the attacker changes their approach to grab the neck or strike the head *(Figure 9.12)*.

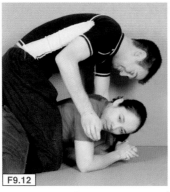

F9.12   F9.13

2. Bring one knee over one of the attacker's legs to pin it down and prevent the attacker from sprawling *(Figure 9.13)*.
3. Push into the ground with your forearms, raising your hips to destabilize your attacker forward. Then turn in the direction of your attacker's pinned leg to roll them over *(Figure 9.14)*.

F9.14

F9.15

4. The attacker may let go of the wrists and post their arm to prevent from being rolled over. If they do, circle the arm with your arm and hold it tight while you re-attempt the roll-over *(Figure 9.14–9.15)*.

F9.16

F9.17

5. If you lose control of your attacker's leg, keep turning your body. This will turn your position into a standard mount, which is an easier position from which to defend *(Figure 9.16–9.17)*.

6. As you come around after successfully rolling the attacker over, strike the groin either with your elbow or your hand, whichever is more natural from your new position.

7. Control the legs with your arms, spreading them out to prevent kick attacks as you get to your feet *(Figure 9.18)*.

F9.18

Defense: Ground and Pound

This attack is particularly dangerous because the base of the skull is exposed. It is also difficult to see the strikes coming. If the attacker is on your back but is not apparently attacking with his hands and arms (i.e. trying to choke you or hold you), you should react as though you are going to get hit for safety's sake. Speed is of the utmost importance because a single solid blow to the base of the skull is enough to knock a person out and potentially cause brain damage, depending on the level of force used.

F9.19

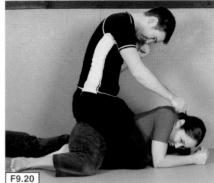

F9.20

1. Turtle up onto your forearms raising your shoulders up as high as they'll go *(Figure 9.19)*.

2. Bring one knee up over one of the attacker's legs to pin it down and prevent the attacker from sprawling *(Figure 9.20)*.

3. Push into the ground with your forearms, raising your hips to destabilize the attacker. Then turn in the direction of his pinned leg rolling him over *(Figure 9.21–9.23)*.

F9.21

F9.22

F9.23

F9.24

4. The attacker may post their arm to prevent from being rolled over. If they do, circle the arm with your arm and hold it tight while you re-attempt the roll over *(Figure 9.22– 9.23)*.

5. After successfully rolling the attacker over, strike their groin either with your elbow or your hand, whichever is more natural in your new position *(Figure 9.24)*.

6. Control the legs with your arms, spreading them out to prevent kick attacks as you get to your feet.

7. If you lose control of your attacker's leg, keep turning your body anyway. This will turn your position into a standard mount, which is an easier position from which to defend.

Defense: Headlock (Belly Down)

This can be a very difficult position to defend from because the attacker is more stable, can apply more weight on their victim, and can more easily control or apply pressure to the neck and head. Attacks to vital targets (what limited ones are available) are likely to be necessary to improve your defensive position, especially if you are considerably smaller than your attacker.

1. Drop your chin and raise your shoulders. This action should be done very aggressively to prevent the attacker from wriggling their arm in to access your throat or carotid arteries *(Figure 9.25)*.

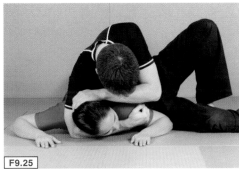

F9.25

F9.26

F9.27

2. Attack whatever vital targets are available. If you manage to tuck your chin fully, you should be able to bite the forearm *(Figure 9.26)*. Depending on the length of your arms relative to your attacker's size, you may be able to bring your arm around to strike and/or grab the testicles, or failing that, you may also attack the sensitive skin around the inner thighs by pinching and twisting or digging in with your nails *(Figure 9.27)*. People with shorter arms may also be able to elbow their attacker's ribs.

Turtled body position without the attacker.

3. Turtle up onto your forearms and your inside knee then turn your body toward your attacker, away from the choking arm *(Figure 9.28)*.

4. One of two things may happen. A slimmer person will hopefully create enough space to roll over onto their back, resulting in a standard scarf hold/ headlock position, which is much easier position against which to defend *(Figure 9.30–9.31)*. A broader individual may simply shift their attacker's body weight as they roll and end up on top.

CHAPTER 10

Defending Against an Attacker Kneeling Between Your Legs, Belly Down

In the last chapter, you learned to deal with the disadvantageous position of defending against a person attacking you from on top of your back. Dealing with an attacker kneeling between your legs while you are belly down has similar disadvantages. Depending on the way they attack you it can be just as difficult if not more so. In this chapter, you'll learn to deal with the unique challenges you face from this position.

The Nature of the Attack

You are in a compromised position in this situation, but not necessarily as compromising as positions in which you are mounted from the rear, at least not from a tactical defense point of view. This position is one that is more likely to be used to control the victim so the attacker can attempt rape or some other form of sexual assault. If you end up in this position, it is probably after having been stunned or knocked out, or overpowered.

Similar to being mounted from the rear, this position is dangerous because you have to fight gravity coupled with the weight of your attacker, and you must do so using backward locomotive actions, which are not as natural as forward ones. Defensively, it is more difficult to use your arms to strike out at an attacker's vital targets. Body shifting techniques are also more difficult due to the use of backward locomotion. That being said, the defender may be able to make better use of their legs, depending on how the attacker is holding them down and applying their weight.

Because you're so vulnerable in this situation, as with any position in which you are being attacked from the rear, to have the best chances of escape, it is imperative to react quickly and aggressively to catch the attacker off guard.

Body Shifting Principles to Keep in Mind

Turtling is the only type of body shifting that can be used when defending against an attacker kneeling between your legs while you are belly-down (see page 38 for turtling practice drills). You must use the ground for leverage using your elbows/forearms and knees to destabilize your attacker and gain a more favorable position from which to defend or to simply escape. In addition to standard body shifting techniques, you can enhance your defensive capability by using your legs to shift your attacker's balance so that you can reverse their position.

Vital Targets to Attack

Much the same as when dealing with an attacker mounted on your back, there are fewer vital targets to attack from this position than from positions in which you are facing the attacker. There are some scenarios in which you could reach behind and grab the groin or pinch and twist sensitive areas such as the inner thigh or the love handles, but these targets may be out of reach or otherwise difficult to access and use effectively. Furthermore, you will likely still need to bring your arms back in front of to use turtling to destabilize the attacker. Biting has the best chance of distracting an attacker if the arms are close enough to your mouth to be accessed. Because there are so few vital targets accessible from this position, you have the best chance of escape using body shifting enhanced by the use your legs for greater control to gain a more favorable position in which more effective options are available.

Defense: Two Hands on Neck

From this position it's harder for the attacker to get the hands around the victim's throat to cut off breathing unless the neck is very small and the attacker's hands are very large. That being said, there is a risk that the attacker could simply slam the victim's head against the ground.

F10.1   F10.2

1. Turtle up onto your forearms while dropping your chin and raising your shoulders to defend against strangulation *(Figure 10.1–10.2)*. This position also makes it more difficult for the attacker to slam your head into the ground, while giving you a point of leverage to help destabilize the attacker.

2. Hook your ankles together and squeeze your legs in, pushing the knees together to remove your attacker's base *(Figure 10.3–10.4)*.

3. Push into the ground with your forearms, turning your hips to the side to destabilize your attacker. A smaller person usually needs to turn more explosively to do this successfully *(Figure 10.5)*.

4. The attacker may let go of the neck and post their arm to prevent from being rolled. If they do, circle the arm with your arm and hold it tight while you re-attempt the roll over *(Figure 10.6–10.7)*.

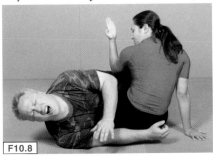
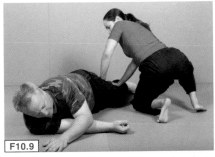

5. As you come around after successfully rolling the attacker over, strike their lateral femoral area with your elbow as a follow-up to give you a better opportunity to get to your feet so you can escape *(Figure 10.8)*.

6. Control the legs with your body weight through your arms as you get to your feet *(Figure 10.9)*.

Defense: Arm Around Neck

F10.10   F10.11

1. Turtle up onto your forearms, dropping your chin and raising your shoulders up as high as they'll go to take the pressure off your throat. If you are able to, bite your attacker's arm to help loosen the grip *(Figure 10.10–10.11)*.

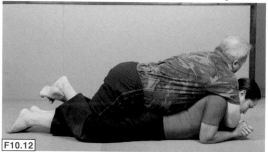

F10.12   F10.13

F10.14   F10.15

2. Hook your ankles together and squeeze your legs in, pushing the knees together to remove your attacker's base *(Figure 10.12–10.13)*.
3. Push into the ground with your forearms, turning your hips to the side to destabilize your attacker. Since the head is closer in this position, add an elbow strike to their head area as you turn to help *(Figure 10.14)*.
4. As you continue to turn over, add any additional strike that is available to you. An open palm strike to the nose is shown here *(Figure 10.15)*.

5. Follow your momentum through to get to your feet. Drive your knee into your attacker's ribs or solar plexus if necessary as you get to your feet to ensure your escape *(Figure 10.16–10.18)*.

Defense: One Hand on Each Wrist

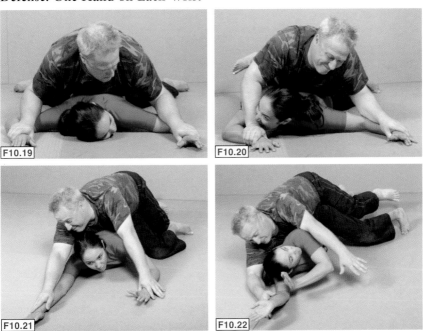

1. If the wrists are close enough to the head, attempt to bite one of the attacker's wrists to distract him. Follow up by turtling up onto one knee and reaching forward with your opposite arm *(Figure 10.19–10.22)*.
2. Push off with your bent knee, turning in the direction of the reaching arm. As you turn into the attacker, add an elbow strike toward their head to help roll them over *(Figure 10.23–10.24)*.

3. As you continue to turn over, add any additional strike like the open palm strike to the nose is shown here *(Figure 10.25)*.
4. Follow your momentum through to get to your feet. Drop your knee into your attacker's ribs or solar plexus if necessary as you get to your feet to ensure your escape *(Figure 10.27)*.

CHAPTER 11

Defending Against Side Controlling Positions

In the last couple of chapters, you learned to deal with a standing attacker that has managed to get control of you from the rear when you're belly down. Now we're going to look at defending against side controlling positions. This type of position may not seem as dangerous or as difficult to deal with at first glance, but if used well, a side controlling position is quite versatile, allowing the attacker to effectively control you with their weight while maneuvering with their entire body.

The Nature of the Attack

When an attacker has taken a side control position, they are in a dominant position with gravity on their side. If your attacker is a grappler and is familiar with this position, they can easily shift between different types of side controlling positions and even switch sides without taking their weight off your chest. They can also create opportunities to put you in a variety of arm locks. This adaptability can make it hard for you, as a defender, to get out from the bottom if your attacker is skilled. That is why it is important to have a variety of different types of tactics for defending against side controlling positions so that you too can adapt to give yourself the best chances of escape. That being said, if the attacker is unskilled or not used to non-competitive tactics, it can be a lot easier to create opportunities to escape. If you find yourself on the bottom of a side controlling position, it is important that you remain calm and try to stay relaxed. This helps make your body movements more difficult to predict, making it harder for your attacker to anticipate and adapt.

Body Shifting Principles to Keep in Mind

Due to the adaptability of side controlling positions, both bridging and rolling, as well as shrimping play a part in your defensive strategy against them. Bridging and/or rolling can be used to shift your position in ways that can help you escape, or in some cases, roll the attacker's weight off you entirely. Shrimping, on the other hand, can help you create the space you need to improve your defensive position. If the attacker has submission grappling experience, there's a good chance you'll need to use a combination of bridging and rolling, as well as shrimping.

Vital Targets to Attack

Depending on the type of side controlling position used, as well as your own position on the underside of the attacker, you'll find that different targets are accessible. If your hands are free to access it, a wide variety of head targets may be available to you, including the eyes, ears, nose, chin, hair, skull, temporal nerve or mandibular angle.

In some situations, you'll find you can access targets on the torso and legs. You may have the option to elbow the ribs or lateral femoral area, bite the nipple or love handles, or if you have a hand free, you may be able to grab and squeeze the groin.

Make use of whatever targets present themselves, but be ready to switch targets should your attacker successfully counter your attack or switch positions.

Defense: Scarf Hold

1. Free your arm from under your attacker's armpit and deliver a palm strike under your attacker's chin. If you find it difficult to free your arm, try biting into the arm that is controlling your neck *(Figure 11.1)*.
2. Adding your other hand for reinforcement, push the chin and head back as far as your reach allows *(Figure 11.2)*.

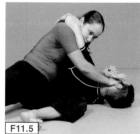

3. Continue to push as you sit up, drawing your legs to the side to create space for your attacker as you roll them onto their side as you come to your knees *(Figure 11.3–11.5)*.

F11.6

F11.7

F11.8

4. Strike your attacker's exposed ribs with your elbow *(Figure 11.6)*.
5. From behind their shoulder and at the top of their leg near the hip, push your attacker fully onto their side to control them as you get to your feet *(Figure 11.7–11.8)*.

Variation for Short Reach

F11.9

F11.10

F11.11

F11.12

1. If you lack the reach or upper body strength to take your attacker's weight off you enough to sit up, once you have their head pushed back as far as it will go, swing your outside leg over their head placing your heel under their chin *(Figure 11.9)*.

2. Driving with the strength of your whole leg under their chin, peel your attacker's weight off your body. As you do so, draw your opposite leg to the side so you don't pin your leg under your attacker's weight *(Figure 11.10–11.11)*.

3. Strike your attacker's exposed ribs with your elbow *(Figure 11.12)*.

4. From behind their shoulder and at the top of their leg, push your attacker onto their side to control them as you get to your feet.

Defense: Scarf Hold—Hug and Roll Variation

This alternative defense may be preferred in certain cases. People with broader bodies relative to their attacker may find this an easier option. It may also be used if you can't free your arm from under your attacker's arm pit, or if your attacker has committed too much of their weight over your body rather than keeping it centered on your chest.

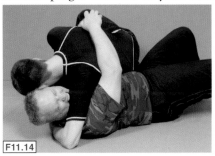

1. Bite the arm that is controlling your neck. Alternatively, you may be able to grab and twist your attacker's love handles *(Figure 11.14)*.

2. Grab your wrist, hugging your attacker low on their body. Bridge your hips up and shift them closer to your attacker's body *(Figure 11.16)*.

3. Once in position, bridge your hips up more aggressively, drawing your attacker's body over your own body with your arms *(Figure 11.17–11.18)*.

F11.19   F11.20

4. Roll your attacker over onto their side as you come to your knees.

F11.21   F11.22

5. Drive your elbow into your attacker's ribs. This is important to prevent them hanging on to your head and trying to roll you. If you don't do this quickly enough, be prepared to shoot your arms forward to post so you can maintain your position *(Figure 11.21–11.22)*.

6. From behind their shoulder and at the top of their leg near the hip, push your attacker fully onto their side to control them as you get to your feet *(Figure 11.23)*.

F11.23

Defense: Scarf Hold (Head Tucked Down)

If your attacker's head is tucked down, the earlier defenses featured in this book may be difficult. Try this option instead.

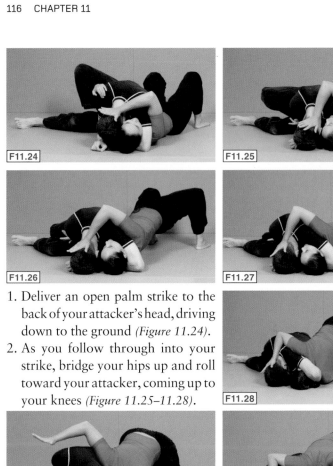

1. Deliver an open palm strike to the back of your attacker's head, driving down to the ground *(Figure 11.24)*.
2. As you follow through into your strike, bridge your hips up and roll toward your attacker, coming up to your knees *(Figure 11.25–11.28)*.

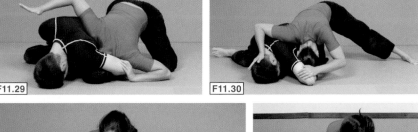

3. If your head is still stuck in the attacker's arm, keep hitting them in the back of the head with your open palm to loosen him up then pull your head out pushing from their head and the back of their arm *(Figure 11.29–11.31)*.
4. If your attacker is still a threat, deliver a knee kick to your attacker's kidney or ribs before getting to your feet *(Figure 11.32)*.

Defense: Side Control—One Knee In

1. Attack any vital target that is accessible from your position. Different targets may be available, depending on their body type and on their arm positioning. If your arms are up, you can elbow your attacker in the ribs or attack their eyes. If your arms are under their body, you may be able to grab and squeeze their testicles *(Figure 11.33–11.36)*.

2. Once your attacker is distracted, push on their hip with the hand that's closest, shrimping onto your side *(Figure 11.37)*.

3. Feed your inside knee under their body to establish a guard position. Once in the guard, use techniques found in chapter 8 to escape the position *(Figure 11.38–11.39)*.

Defense: Side Control—Both Knees In

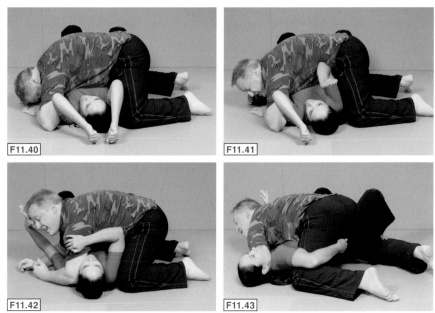

1. If your arms are up in this position, attack any vital targets that are available to you to either force a changed position or to give you an opportunity to get your arms under their body. Different targets may be available, depending on their body type and on their arm positioning. For example, you may be able to elbow their ribs or attack their eyes *(Figure 11.40–11.43)*.

2. If starting with your arms under your attacker's body, distract them by grabbing and squeezing their testicles. Alternatively, you can try pinching their inner thigh or grabbing and twisting a love handle *(Figure 11.44)*.

3. Once you have sufficiently distracted your attacker, bridge your hips up explosively, pulling your body out from under theirs. To get the necessary explosiveness, you may need to lift your feet up and slam them into the ground if you're a smaller person *(Figure 11.45–11.46)*.

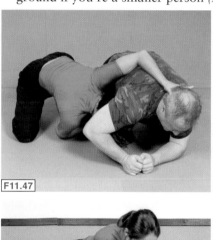

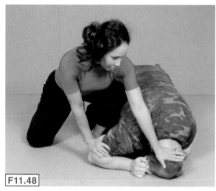

4. As you escape, roll in the direction of your attacker, coming up to your knees, putting your weight on their back for control *(Figure 11.47–11.49)*.

5. If your attacker is still a threat, deliver a knee kick to your attacker's ribs then get to your feet *(Figure 11.50)*.

CHAPTER 12

Defending Against Bottom Controlling Positions

In the last chapter, you learned a few options for defending against side controlling positions that are commonly used by submission grapplers. Now we're going to look at another type of position favored by sport grapplers: bottom controlling positions. Unlike side controlling positions, which can be used to effectively control a person on the ground in both the sporting arena and on the street, bottom controlling positions are considerably less useful against someone who doesn't fight back within a rule system, and pose much greater dangers in a street context, which makes life easier for you as a defender.

The Nature of the Attack

When an attacker has taken a bottom control position, they don't have gravity on their side, but they are able use their legs to control you, particularly if the attacker has any submission grappling training under their belt. This is commonly known as the "guard" position. If the legs are hooked at the ankles around the back of the defender, it is called a "closed guard." If only one leg is wrapped up by someone elses legs, it is a "half guard." If the legs are completely open, it is known as an "open guard."

If your goal is to escape, the open guard does not pose much of a threat to you. You can just get up whenever you like since the legs aren't controlling you. The only real risk is that the attacker could grab your arms to try and keep you down, or they could kick you as you get up. Attacks to vital targets can be easily applied to get your arms free, and as you get up, you want to make sure you keep the legs controlled as you get to your feet. If necessary, you also have the option to strike the groin, an easy target from this position.

Closed guards require a little more effort as you need to take some action to separate the legs so you can free yourself *(Figure 12.1)*. The attacker can make this more difficult by grabbing your neck and pulling it down to their chest. The greatest threat to you on the receiving end of a closed guard is that your attacker may attempt to sweep you to put themselves in a more dominant position, or try to put you into some sort of submission, whether it is a neck restraint or a joint lock. Be sure to read through Chapter 13 and 15 for ways of dealing with these types of attacks. Once free of the leg grip, you also need to be ready to defend against kicks as you attempt to get to your feet.

The half guard is a closed guard in which only one leg is trapped *(Figure 12.2)*. It is generally not a preferred position and is usually only used to prevent someone from passing one's guard fully in a submission grappling context. It is unlikely that you would end up in a half guard on the street for this reason, so long as you're defending yourself to escape rather than to "win the fight." If you do end up in this position, it is fairly easy to get out since your attacker has so many vulnerable vital targets.

It is important to not let yourself get wrapped up in a submission grappling approach to dealing with the guard when you're on the street. Passing the guard as is commonly practiced in

F12.1

F12.2

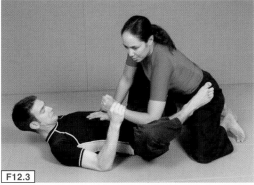

F12.3

competitive circles takes more time and effort to free yourself, and once past the guard, even though you are in a better controlling position, you're still on the ground and vulnerable to attacks from any friends your attacker may have who are willing to join the fight *(Figure 12.3)*. You may find exceptions to this rule though if you are a law enforcement professional. If you have a partner for back up and not at risk of being attacked by other people, passing the guard so you can control the suspect more easily and get them into a position in which you can handcuff them.

Body Shifting Principles to Keep in Mind

F12.4

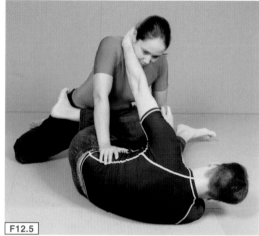

F12.5

Body shifting does not play any role in this context other than being mindful of the body shifting your attacker may use. If your attacker shrimps onto their side, they could be setting up a sweep of some sort. To prevent this from happening, maintain a strong base by keeping your knees as far apart as possible. In addition, try to keep your

F12.6

arms unrestrained so you can post your arm to form a tripod if necessary in order to recover your base *(Figure 12.4–12.6)*.

Vital Targets to Attack

There are a number of vulnerable targets that can be utilized when on the receiving end of a guard. The groin is right in front of you and can be easily accessed. If the guard is closed tight though, you may not necessarily be able to attack the testicles effectively from the top side. In this case, you can go around the legs and behind the body to access the testicles from the rear. Another option is to pinch the inner thigh. Another alternative is to drive the tip of your elbow into the anterior femoral area to cause pain to your attacker. Bear in mind, however, an experienced submission grappler may be desensitized to these types of attacks as they are commonly used in their trade.

If being drawn forward, you can drive your elbow into your attacker's solar plexus or ribs. If your attacker has fully broken your posture and drawn your head down into their chest, your hands may be free to attack vital targets on the head such as the eyes, nose, ears, throat, or mandibular angle. These targets are all potentially accessible from a half guard position as well.

Defense: Closed Guard

1. Maintain a strong upright posture with your chin up, engaging your neck muscles while keeping a hand pushing into the attacker's solar plexus. The hand push makes it difficult for the attacker to reach up to grab your neck to pull you down *(Figure 12.7)*. Even if their arms are long enough to grab onto your neck, by keeping your chin up and neck muscles engaged, it is fairly easy to resist *(Figure 12.8)*. If your chin is down *(Figure 12.9)*, it is much easier for the attacker to pull you down.

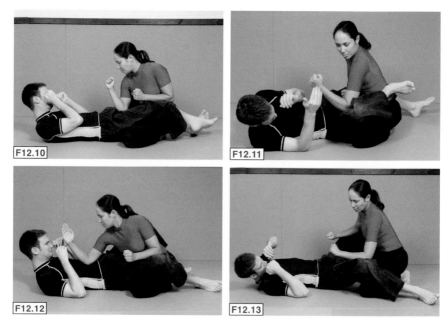

2. Distract your attacker by attacking a vital target. This can be done in multiple ways, be it dropping an elbow into the groin (which can be done even if your attacker has grabbed on to your wrists), driving your elbow into their anterior femoral, pinching the inner thigh or dropping an elbow into their solar plexus *(Figure 12.10–12.13)*.

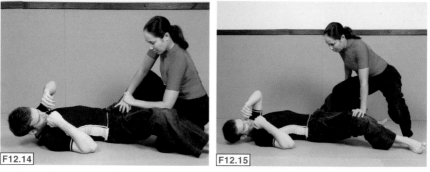

3. Once the leg grip has been loosened, force the legs apart with your arms.
4. Hold the legs apart and, if necessary, deliver one last parting strike to the groin to ensure they don't continue their attack as you try to escape *(Figure 12.14–12.15)*.

Defense: Closed Guard—Head Pulled Down

If your attacker catches you off guard and manages to pull your head down to their chest, use this defense.

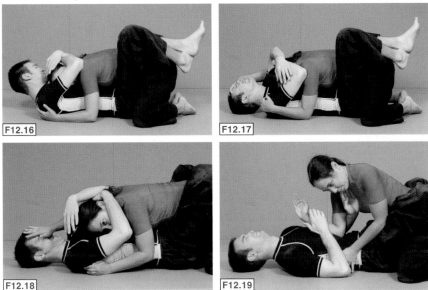

1. Using your hands attack any vital targets you can access in the head/neck area. The eyes (shown here), nose, ears and throat are all good potential targets *(Figure 12.16–12.18)*.
2. Once distracted, pull your head out of their weakened grip. Driving an elbow into the solar plexus as you posture yourself up *(Figure 12.19)*.
3. Once fully postured up, follow the directions from defense against closed guard shown previously.

Defense: Half Guard

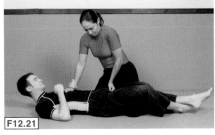

1. Deliver any strikes that are accessible from your position to loosen the leg grip. This can be done in multiple ways, be it attacking the groin, driving an elbow into the lateral femoral area or the ribs, grabbing and squeezing a love handle, are all potential options *(Figure 12.20–12.21)*.

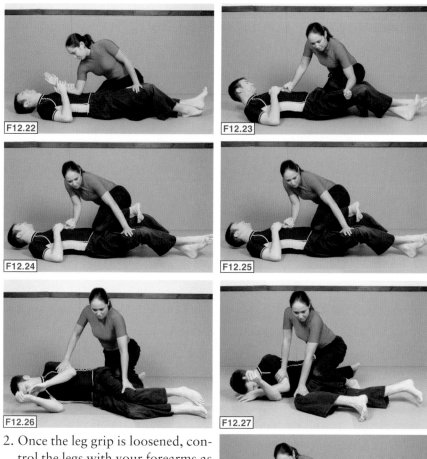

2. Once the leg grip is loosened, control the legs with your forearms as you draw your knee up through the grip. Your attacker may try to re-establish his half guard as you try to free your leg. Leading with your knee makes this harder for them to do *(Figure 12.22–12.25).*

3. Once your leg is completely free, push into your attacker's closest knee and stack it onto their other knee to control the legs. If necessary, drive an elbow into your attacker's ribs as you get up on your feet to keep them from attempting to re-engage their attack *(Figure 12.26–12.28).*

CHAPTER 13

Applying Neck Restraints

In the last chapter, you learned a few options for defending against bottom controlling positions, which are commonly used by submission grapplers. The bottom controlling position commonly known as the guard position can present a variety of hazards when dealing with practiced grapplers. One such hazard is neck restraints. If someone uses a neck restraint on you with intent to harm, there is the potential for serious injury, or even death, so it is important to learn skills for defending against them. To learn to defend against these types of attacks, you must first learn to apply them. If you and your training partners aren't particularly skilled at applying them, you won't fully understand what it takes to defend against them. Learning to apply neck restraints also helps you understand how they work and where the weaknesses are in their application. So even if you don't use the neck restraint defenses presented in Chapter 14, it still helps develop your ability to improvise defenses against these neck restraints, especially so if you practice live ground grappling.

There may also be some scenarios in which it might make sense to use certain types of neck restraints to subdue an attacker in order to create an opportunity to escape. For the most part though, there are many other defensive options that are easier to learn and use. If you're in law enforcement, certain types of neck restraints may prove useful for subduing suspects that pose a serious threat to you and/or other people.

The Dangers of Using Neck Restraints in Self-Defense

Neck restraints may seem like an effective way of subduing an attacker, however there are a number of risks that can be associated with their application. No matter what kind of neck restraint you use on the ground, you become tied up in dealing with a single attacker. If someone else steps in to help your attacker, you're in a vulnerable position. On top of that, if your attacker is bigger or stronger than you, it can be difficult to control them sufficiently in order to apply a neck restraint effectively, even if you have great technique.

If you choose to use a neck restraint against an attacker, it is much safer and more effective from a self-defense point of view to use sanguineous restraints rather than respiratory restraints or neck cranks. This is because of the body's different reactions to these three different types of restraints.

Respiratory Restraints

There are a number of factors that make respiratory neck restraints particularly dangerous. They involve applying pressure to the trachea, around the larynx and hyoid bone. There is always the potential that you could cause damage to the internal tissue causing swelling that could result in self-strangulation that occurs even after the neck restraint is released. If the person dies, you may find yourself in a situation in which you have to defend yourself legally for killing a person, even if your intention was only to subdue him sufficiently so that you could escape.

If your intention is in fact to subdue a subject, there are further reasons why you should steer away from respiratory neck restraints. Due to the high levels of discomfort created by respiratory neck restraints, the subject is very aware of the feeling of being choked, putting them in the mental state of fighting for their life. This can result in an adrenalin dump that increases their strength and will to resist.

Even if you're able to keep the neck restraint applied on the trachea, there is a good chance that you would have to keep dealing with a struggling assailant for as a long as 4-5 minutes. This is because of the way the body works. The trachea supplies the lungs with air inhaled through the nose and mouth. Pressure to the trachea can quickly and effectively prevent inhalation of air to the lungs, but the brain is not immediately deprived of oxygen. This is because there is still oxygenated blood in the circulatory system, continuing to flow to the brain, which is why it can take so long to render a subject unconscious. Even if you manage to keep your attacker in a respiratory restraint long enough to end the struggle, there is a good chance of causing enough damage to the internal tissue within that time that it could result in their death.

Neck Cranks

In MMA/BJJ competition circles, neck cranks are taught as spinal lock submission techniques applied by pulling, bending, twisting or elongating the neck beyond its normal ranges of rotation, causing hyper-extension, hyper-flexion, hyper-rotation or extension-distraction of the cervical spine. They are applied to cause enough pain and/or discomfort to get opponents to submit by tapping out. This could play out very differently when used in a non-competitive context.

If your subject is unwilling to submit and leave you alone, you would have essentially two options: 1) cause enough injury to the neck that they are no longer a threat or 2) release them and deal with them another way. If you decide to cause injury to the neck, you may find yourself having to justify why you had to use lethal force in court, as a neck crank fully applied has the potential to kill the subject or cause a permanent injury with serious life implications such as paralysis.

Sanguineous Restraints

Of the three types of neck restraints, sanguineous restraints are the best for controlling a subject with the least risk of causing serious injury. Pressure is applied to the carotid arteries located under the ears on each side of the neck. Applying a sanguineous restraint can greatly reduce the flow of oxygenated blood to the brain, and can cause unconsciousness in less than 10 seconds. Unconsciousness usually lasts anywhere between 5 and 30 seconds. If you apply this type of restraint, never hold it on any longer than it takes to render someone unconscious, as this has the potential to cause blindness, brain damage or even death.

Even though sanguineous restraints are the best choice of the three types of neck restraints for controlling an attacker, you should still exercise caution in its use. If your attacker is bigger or stronger than you, you may find it difficult to establish enough control to apply sanguineous restraints effectively. Even if you are able to apply it effectively, you must still be wary of the level of force you are using to subdue your attacker as there are always risks of serious injury and even death when doing any form of attack to the neck area. Many law enforcement professionals are taught that they should only use sanguineous restraints, such as the rear naked choke, when subjects are demonstrating a threat of grievous bodily harm or death. If a subject does not regain consciousness after 30 seconds, they are also taught to administer first aid and to call for medical assistance.

If you're a civilian who used a neck restraint in self-defense and it resulted in injury or unconsciousness, you may not necessarily think about calling for medical assistance for your downed attacker. Even if you're concerned about the attacker's welfare, you may not want to apply first aid for fear of being put at further risk. Calling 911 (emergency services) is usually the best choice either way, as the downed attacker (or his friends) may still pose a threat, and downed attacker will be given the opportunity to receive medical attention for his injuries.

Training Tips for Working with Neck Restraints

For safety in training, always apply neck restraints with slow even pressure to allow your partner enough time to tap. When applying any sort of neck restraint, always release the pressure immediately when your partner taps. If training to use a sanguineous restraint to subdue an attacker, when your partner taps, back off the pressure for a moment while keeping the neck under control before releasing the neck restraint altogether. If you intend to use sanguineous restraints in real situations, you don't want to be in the habit of completely releasing your hold when your subject taps because then you'll have to start all over again.

Triangle from Guard

The triangle is a sanguineous restraint using the legs to cut off the blood supply to the brain. It is demonstrated here with the left leg up, but of course, you can reverse sides for all these instructions to apply the restraint with the right leg up.

 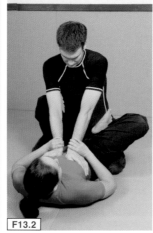 

F13.1   F13.2   F13.3

1. Control your partner's arms by either grabbing their wrists or the sleeves near to the wrists *(Figure 13.1)*.
2. If in a closed guard, release the guard, placing your right foot on your partner's left hip. Bridge your hips up, bringing your left leg around your partner's neck *(Figure 13.2–13.3)*.

F13.4   F13.5

3. Break your partner's posture down, drawing their head toward your right and their left arm across their body *(Figure 13.4–13.5)*.

F13.6

F13.7

F13.8

F13.9

4. Hook your left foot behind your right knee, bending your right knee. Your partner is now enclosed in a triangle, with your left thigh applying pressure to their right carotid artery, their own left arm applying pressure to their left carotid artery, and your left calf closing off the triangle behind their head. Squeeze with your legs to increase the amount of pressure until your partner taps *(Figure 13.6)*.

5. If you aren't able to apply quite enough pressure to get your partner to submit, grab your partner's right leg near the knee and turn your body clockwise to improve your angle of application *(Figure 13.7)*.

6. If you are still unable to get your partner to submit, you can also try pulling their head forward to further increase the effectiveness *(Figure 13.8–13.9)*.

Triangle from Mount

1. The best set-up for a triangle from mount is if your partner tries to hook your leg when you raise up on your foot from mount. If your partner doesn't do this, you could still work your way into this position with a little effort *(Figure 13.10)*.

2. If your left leg is up, draw your partner's head forward using your right hand, while drawing your left leg behind their neck *(Figure 13.11–13.14)*.

3. Force your partner's left arm higher pushing with your right thigh. Grab this arm by the wrist and draw it across your partner's chest *(Figure 13.15)*.

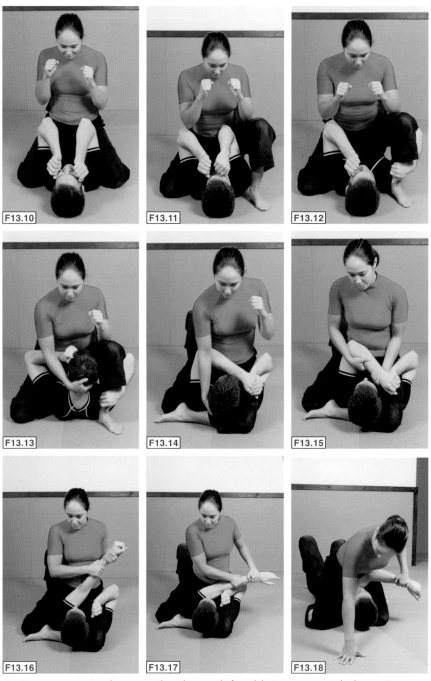

F13.10

F13.11

F13.12

F13.13

F13.14

F13.15

F13.16

F13.17

F13.18

4. Come up to your knees and tuck your left ankle into your right knee. Squeeze with your legs to apply pressure, decreasing pressure when your partner taps. For safety, do this action slowly until they tap *(Figure 13.16–13.18)*.

5. If you are unable to get enough pressure from this position, roll over onto your back and use the techniques in 5-6 of "Triangle from Guard" *(Figure 13.19–13.20)*.

Guillotine

The guillotine is a respiratory restraint using the forearm to cut off the air supply at the trachea. It is demonstrated here using the right arm, but you can reverse sides for all these instructions to apply the restraint with the left arm.

From All Fours

1. Leading from the shoulder for the tightest application, wrap your right arm around your partner's head, drawing your forearm up into their trachea *(Figure 13.21–13.22)*.
2. Grab your wrist with your left hand and apply pressure to the back of your partner's neck by leaning your weight into your right shoulder. This may cause enough pressure to get your partner to tap *(Figure 13.23)*.

F13.24   F13.25

3. If there isn't enough pressure for a submission, roll onto your back. From here, close your guard by hooking your ankles together behind your partner's back *(Figure 13.24–13.25)*.

4. Lift your hips up to improve your leverage so you can apply more pressure to the restraint until your partner taps. For safety while training, do this action slowly until they tap.

From Guard

F13.26   F13.27   F13.28

1. The best time to apply a guillotine from guard is when your partner takes their hands off your body for whatever reason. If they don't you may still be able to grab their wrist and draw it off your body *(Figure 13.27)*.

2. Sit up as high as you can and wrap your right arm around your partner's neck, leading from the shoulder for the tightest application, grabbing their right wrist with your left hand *(Figure 13.28)*.

F13.29   F13.30   F13.31

3. Lean your body back and lift your hips until your partner taps. For safety while training, do this action slowly until they tap *(Figure 13.29–13.31)*.

Rear Naked Choke

The best choices of sanguineous restraints for subduing an attacker are ones that are applied from the rear, like the rear naked choke. This is because it is harder to defend against attacks from the rear, increasing the chances of a successful application. The rear naked choke is demonstrated here using the right arm in front, but of course, you can reverse sides for all these instructions to apply the restraint with the left arm in front.

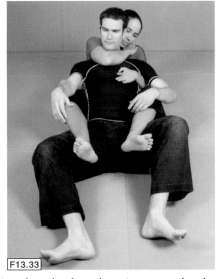

F13.32   F13.33

1. Control your partner's body by leaning them back and getting your "hooks in," wrapping their legs with your own, digging your heels into your knees or thighs to control their legs and hips. Wrap your right arm around your partner's neck, elbow close to the chin *(Figure 13.32–13.33)*.

F13.34   F13.35

2. Keeping your left arm behind your partner's left shoulder, quickly draw it up so that your right hand tucks inside the crease of your left elbow. Then draw your left forearm and hand behind your partner's head with your left elbow controlling your partner's left shoulder. Tuck your head in tight to your partner's head *(Figure 13.34–13.35)*.

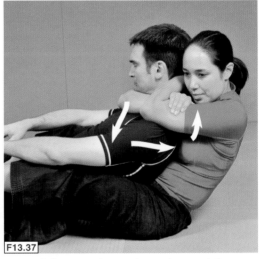

F13.36   F13.37

3. Apply pressure by drawing your right arm down, in and up while your left hand pushes into the head with the blade. For safety while training, do this action slowly until they tap *(Figure 13.36–13.37)*.

CHAPTER 14

Defending Against Common Neck Restraints

In the last chapter, you learned some of the most common neck restraints used by submission grapplers. Now that you have some understanding of how they work, you can learn the most important thing about them for street defense purposes; how to defend against them. Getting caught on the receiving end of a neck restraint can be very dangerous, in some cases lethal, so it's well worth learning the defensive tactics in this chapter.

The Nature of the Attack

Neck restraints commonly used in submission grappling are not as commonly used on the street. That being said, BJJ and MMA are among the most popular martial arts in western countries, particularly ones in North America. While the vast majority of people training in these styles do so with only an interest in learning a new skill and better themselves in some way, there is always a chance you could face someone using these techniques for malicious purposes, such as when the person is drunk and not thinking clearly about his actions, engaging in macho bravado to show off to his friends, etc.

The most common forms of neck restraints involve either cutting off the blood flow to the brain from the carotid arteries or cutting off respiration by blocking the trachea. A third class of neck restraints known as neck cranks are different. They involve applying pressure to the spine to cause pain. If applied rapidly, they could be used to severely injure or even break the neck, which could lead to paralysis or death. The best way to prevent any of these types of attacks is to be ready for them before they happen, dealing with them before they are fully applied. The later into the neck restraint you get caught, the harder it is to get out of it. If you note that your attacker moves as a skilled grappler does, you should be ready to defend against neck restraints.

F14.1

While the tactics for avoiding being choked are a little different depending on the form of neck restraint, there are certain commonalities to keep in mind. The most important principle is to be ready to obstruct anything that could be used to apply pressure around your neck. At the earliest stages of defense, this can mean keeping arms or legs in check using your own arms and legs and preventing them from getting close to your neck. It is also important to keep your chin tucked and shoulders up to minimize access to your neck. At later stages of defense, you can use your chin more aggressively, while moving your head and shoulders strategically to block advances on your neck or release pressure from it if a neck restraint is already applied.

In this book, we specifically cover defenses against neck restraints that don't require the use of a *gi* (training uniform). The reason for this is that people don't wear uniforms on the street. There is the possibility that a street jacket could be used to apply neck restraints, but for the most part, they aren't very well suited for this purpose. In the unlikely event that you do face this type of neck restraint, you can still apply the above principles while defending against them.

*Tip: If all else fails, tap out. Don't hesitate to use a submission grappler's training against them. They are trained to release their submission attacks when their "partner" taps out. The more experience they have, the more likely they are to do this, even if they aren't in a training context. While you shouldn't rely on this as a primary defense, if you're stuck and you're in danger of being choked out, it's definitely worth a try.

There are a wide variety of methods for escaping common neck restraints. This book demonstrates a few methods that lend themselves well to combining body shifting with attacks to vital targets, which can be used by people of different body types. But with the variety of methods that are out there, don't hesitate to experiment with a number of methods to see which ones work best for you. If you're consulting submission grappling resources though, remember to make adjustments if you intend to use their techniques for the purposes of a self-defense situation since your goal is not to win a competition, but to escape.

Body Shifting Principles to Keep in Mind

The body shifting principles used to defend against neck restraints are specific to the restraint against which you are defending, and are therefore not covered in chapter 3. They are designed to alleviate the pressure on your neck so that you are not in danger of being choked out, or to make it difficult for your attacker to use their arms, legs, etc, effectively to apply their chosen restraint. More details on this will be covered in the instructional portion on the defenses against each type of neck restraint.

Vital Targets to Attack

It's important to note that attacks to vital targets are more useful earlier in the defense process against neck restraints, before they are fully applied. If you're able to obstruct your attacker's attempt at a neck restraint early on, there are fewer risks involved in using attacks to their vital targets. If you're going for vital targets as a primary technique in a last ditch effort to get out of a choke after it is fully applied, there is a good chance you'll end up unconscious or worse. Unless you're able to completely incapacitate your attacker with an attack to a vital target, you must find a way to release some, if not all the pressure on your neck *before* you attempt to use any vital targets to aid your escape. When it comes to specific vital targets, there are different options against different positions. These will be covered in the instructional portion on the defenses against each type of neck restraint.

Defense: Triangle (Early)

The triangle is most commonly performed from the guard position, though it is possible to apply it from other positions, including the mount, scarf hold, etc. Whatever position you are defending from, the main principles for defending against triangles are fairly similar. In the instructional portion of this book, however, we'll focus primarily on defending against triangle attempts from the guard position since they are more commonly practiced from this position.

F14.2   F14.3   F14.4

1. Maintain a strong upright posture with your chin up, engaging your neck muscles while keeping a hand pushing into the attacker's solar plexus. The hand push makes it difficult for the attacker to reach up to grab your neck to pull you down *(Figure 14.2–14.3)*. Breaking your posture in this way can make it easier for your attacker to position themselves to apply a triangle.
2. To apply a triangle your attacker must open their guard. As soon as they do, get up to your feet while keeping the legs controlled from the inside using your hands and forearms *(Figure 14.4)*.

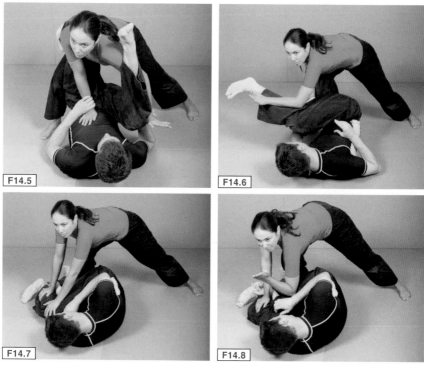

F14.5 F14.6 F14.7 F14.8

3. From the outside of one of the attacker's legs, use your arm to push the legs together and over to the side, stacking them *(Figure 14.5–14.7)*.

4. If necessary, strike the attacker's groin with your hand or drive an elbow into the lateral femoral to keep them from attempting to re-engage the attack *(Figure 14.8)*.

Defense: Triangle (Late)

This method can be used if you're caught off guard and aren't able to stop the triangle before it is fully applied. Once the triangle is locked on with the ankle behind the knee, you have very little time (10 seconds) before you lose consciousness from lack of blood flow to the brain, so you must act fast.

F14.9 F14.10

(**Warning:** Make sure you perform this technique on the side where the leg has wrapped your neck and not the opposite side. Doing this on the opposite side will only serve to tighten the triangle, increasing its effectiveness for your attacker.)

1. Clasp your hands together, while dropping your chin and raising the shoulder on the side of the attacker's leg. Draw the leg into you while leaning forward, compressing it into your attacker's body *(Figure 14.9–14.10)*.
2. Use your outside hand to strike across your attacker's head area with your palm. You can target their ear, jaw or skull. As you strike, drive their head across *(Figure 14.11–14.13)*.

3. As you follow through the strike, stand up and turn your body, placing your outside foot by your attacker's shoulder. As you do so, drive shoulder into your attacker's leg toward their head using your body weight *(Figure 14.14)*.
4. Step across your attacker's head to the opposite side, continuing to turn your body until the triangle releases *(Figure 14.15)*.
5. Press your attacker's legs into the ground to keep them controlled as you step around their body and come to your feet *(Figure 14.16)*.

Defense: Guillotine

Because this is a respiratory restraint attacking the trachea, it is vital to respond to this neck restraint before it is fully applied. If your attacker fully applies this choke with intent to seriously harm you, they could easily damage the internal tissues surrounding the trachea, causing swelling that can result in self-strangulation. Even if your attacker fails to apply sufficient pressure on your trachea to cause damage or block respiration, they could still use this position to apply a neck crank, which has the potential to cause serious injury to your neck that could result in paralysis or death.

1. As your attacker wraps his arm around your neck, drop your chin and raise your shoulders to take some pressure off your throat *(Figure 14.17)*.
2. Jump your legs and hips over to the side of your attacker's body opposite to the choking side, driving your shoulder over their shoulder *(Figure 14.18)*.

3. Turn your face toward the floor keeping your chin dropped, digging it into your attacker's rib cage to keep pressure off your throat *(Figure 14.19)*.
4. Strike across your attacker's head area with your palm. You can target their ear, jaw, or skull. As you strike, drive their head across, positioning your forearm against their neck *(Figure 14.20)*.
5. Pressing your forearm into their neck with one arm and the floor with your opposite hand, pull your head and neck out of your attacker's grip. The harder your attacker tries to hold, the more pressure they will receive in their neck from your forearm, causing pain as it cranks their neck.

6. If your attacker is particularly resilient and does not release their grip, strike targets in their head area, such as the nose or jaw with your palm or elbow, or go for the eyes to further facilitate your escape *(Figure 14.21–14.22)*.

7. Once you're free, immediately step back and away from your attacker.

Defense: Rear Naked Choke

As with the triangle, the earlier you respond in the application of this neck restraint, the easier it is to escape.

1. If an experienced grappler takes control of you from the rear and gets their "hooks in," wrapping your legs with their own, digging their heels into your knees or thighs, there is a strong chance they will attempt this choke. Drop your chin to your chest and raise your shoulders immediately, before they start to wrap their arm around your neck *(Figure 14.23)*.

2. As their forearm comes around your neck, grab it with both hands, pulling it down, and tuck your head to your shoulder on the side that the arm is wrapped, turning your chin away from the arm *(Figure 14.24)*.

3. If you don't react quickly enough and they get their arms fully into position, grab your attacker's forearm, pull down, and dig your chin under their forearm, raising your shoulder as you do so *(Figure 14.25)*. Remember: you only have around 10 seconds to get the pressure off your neck before you start to lose consciousness from lack of blood flow to your brain.

F14.26

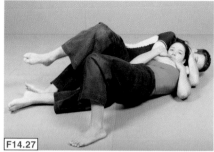
F14.27

4. Bridge your hips and lean to the side opposite your attacker's choking arm. Step over your attacker's leg, scooting your hips across it, putting weight on it to keep it controlled *(Figure 14.26–14.27)*.

5. Pushing with both hands on the opposite leg, shrimp your hips all the way to the other side of the controlled leg *(Figure 14.28)*.

6. Strike the groin while controlling your attacker's free leg with the other hand to help prevent them from re-engaging as you get to your feet *(Figure 14.29–14.30)*.

F14.28

F14.29

F14.30

CHAPTER 15

Applying Joint Locks

In the last couple of chapters, you learned some of the most common neck restraints used by submission grapplers and how to defend against them. Other common attacks used by them involve locking joints in the arms and legs. While joint locks aren't potentially lethal like neck restraints, they do have the potential to cause serious injuries that can take months, even years to heal. As with neck restraints, to learn to defend against these types of attacks, you must first learn to apply them. If you and your training partners aren't particularly skilled at applying them, you won't fully understand what it takes to defend against them. Learning to apply them also helps you understand their mechanics and where the weaknesses are in their application. So even if you don't use the specific defenses taught in chapter 16, it still helps develop your ability to improvise defenses against these joint locks, especially so if you practice live ground grappling.

There may also be some scenarios in which it might make sense to use certain types of joint locks to keep an attacker under control or to injure a joint so that the limb becomes useless in their attack. For the most part though, there are many other defensive options that are easier to learn and use.

The Dangers of Using Joint Locks for Ground Defense

Joint locks may seem like an effective way of subduing or controlling an attacker, but there are a number of risks that are associated with their application. No matter what kind of joint lock you use, you become tied up in dealing with a single attacker on the ground. If someone else steps in to help the attacker, you're in a vulnerable position. On top of that, if your attacker is bigger or stronger than you, it can be difficult to control them sufficiently in order to apply a joint lock effectively, even if you have great technique.

Another issue of concern is that your attacker may not be compliant, even after the application of a joint lock. They may be too drunk or high, or filled with adrenalin to feel the pain associated with the lock or understand its implications. At this point, you would have to make a choice as to whether you'll damage the joint (which you may have to justify later legally) or simply let them go and run the risk that the person will attack you again. Without compliance, joint locks offer no lower level force options for dealing with the attacker. This may not concern you if the stakes are high and your life is at risk, but if it's a friend who has had a bit too much to drink and has just let their emotions get away from them then a joint lock may not be a great choice.

Training Tips for Working with Joint Locks

For safety in training, always apply locks with slow even pressure to allow your partner enough time to tap. When applying any sort of joint lock, always back off the pressure immediately when your partner taps. Don't get in the habit of fully releasing the lock though; otherwise you're training yourself to always release a joint lock when tapped. This is a dangerous habit to have if you ever use joint locks in a real situation. What you do in training is what you'll likely do on the street.

Arm Bar From the Mount

The arm bar is a joint lock that targets the elbow using the hip where it joins the leg as the primary leverage point. Follow this description when applying this lock to your partner's right arm. Reverse all the directions if applying the lock to the left arm.

1. Once you've established mount, try to shift your weight so that it's resting on your partner's chest, rather than his hips. This makes it harder for them to shift your balance *(Figure 15.1)*.

F15.1

F15.2

F15.3

F15.4

2. Many people will simply grab the arm that they intend to arm bar, but this makes it easier for your partner to see it coming and counter it *(Figure 15.2)*.

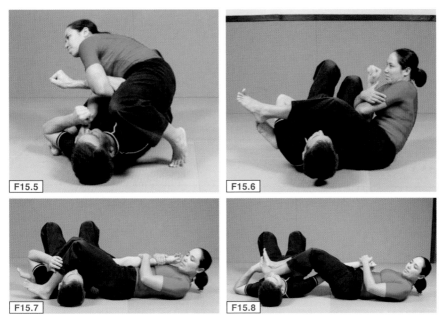

F15.5   F15.6

F15.7   F15.8

It also can become a strength game in order to establish enough control over the arm to put it in an arm bar. Instead, raise your left knee, keeping your weight on your opponent's chest. Wrap your left arm around your partner's right arm at the elbow, holding it tight into your body while hooking your hand around your right hip *(Figure 15.3–15.4)*.

3. Swing your leg over your partner's head around to the opposite side of their body, letting your hips slide down to the base of their shoulder. Keep the hips in tight for the most control *(Figure 15.5–15.6)*.
4. Squeeze your knees together while raising your hips up, drawing your opponent's elbow across your inside thigh. While training, do this action slowly until they tap *(Figure 15.7–15.8)*.

If applying this in a self-defense situation dangerous enough to justify causing serious damage to their elbow, steps 3-4 can be done in one sharp motion.

Arm Bar From the Guard

Follow the description below when applying this lock to your partner's left arm. Reverse all the directions if applying to the right arm.

F15.9

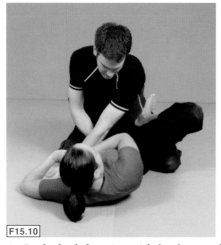

1. Grab the left wrist with both your hands *(Figure 15.10)*. If your partner is wearing a long sleeved uniform, grabbing the sleeve at the wrist can also work. If starting from a closed guard, open your legs and draw the arm across your body while you break your partner's balance forward to your right by pushing from behind their right shoulder with your left leg *(Figure 15.11)*. These movements should be done simultaneously for best effect.

2. Swing your right leg around your partner's head. Squeeze your knees together while raising your hips up, drawing your opponent's elbow across your inside thigh at the hip. For safety while training, do this action slowly until they tap *(Figure 15.12–15.14)*.

3. If you want more control over your partner's body, instead of applying as in step 2, raise your hips and push your partner's upper body with your legs to break their balance and roll them onto their back *(Figure 15.15)*.

4. Squeeze your knees together while raising your hips up, drawing your opponent's elbow across your inside thigh. For safety while training, do this action slowly until they tap *(Figure 15.16)*.

   As mentioned previously, if applying this in a self-defense situation dangerous enough to justify causing serious damage to their elbow, the lock can be applied in one sharp motion.

Kimura From the Guard

The Kimura is a joint lock that targets the shoulder using the arms as the primary leverage point. Follow this description when applying this lock to your partner's right shoulder. Reverse all the directions if applying it to the left shoulder.

1. Grab your partner's right wrist. A great time to do this is when your partner puts their hand on the ground for whatever reason. If they don't, you can still grab their wrist, but you'll have to make sure you have control over it, keeping their hand off your own body, before continuing your attempt to apply this lock *(Figure 15.17)*.

2. If starting from a closed guard, open your legs and put your feet on the ground. Reach behind your partner's right shoulder with your right arm then snake it under and around their right arm, grabbing your left wrist.

As you do this, support your weight on your right foot while allowing your left leg to "float." This allows you to use body leverage rather than muscle engagement to do this more quickly with less energy *(Figure 15.19–15.20).*

3. Lean back and swing your left leg over your partner's back toward their opposite shoulder. This will force their balance forward as you turn your body *(Figure 15.21–15.22).*

4. Maintaining your grip and control over your partner's arm, turn your hips (slowly for safety while training) toward their head. Push into their back with your leg for added leverage. Keeping turning until they tap *(Figure 15.23).*

If applying this in a self-defense situation dangerous enough to justify causing serious damage to their shoulder, this lock can be applied in one sharp motion.

Kimura From Side Control

Follow the description below when applying this lock to your partner's right shoulder. Reverse all the directions if applying it to the left shoulder.

F15.24

F15.25

1. If your partner is smart, they'll start with their arms under your body when on the bottom of the side control. This makes it harder for you to access their arms for locks. They may also have their close knee bent, propped on their opposite thigh to make it harder for you to swing your leg over to take mount *(Figure 15.24)*.
2. Release the head control, bringing your right hand to the opposite side of your partner's body, hugging it tightly around their right arm, placing your hand on their waist *(Figure 15.25)*. You can make this more secure by grabbing onto a belt or even the flesh of their love handle, which can also make for a great distraction as long as you're not following a rule system.

F15.26

F15.27

3. From this position, switch your hips to put yourself into a reverse scarf hold. This will expose your partner's right arm *(Figure 15.26)*.
4. Grab your partner's right wrist with your left hand, pinning it to their body. Slip your right hand under your partner's right arm, grabbing onto your left wrist. Do not wrap your thumb around the wrist. Keep it alongside your fingers for better leverage and control *(Figure 15.27)*.

5. Lift your partner's arm up away from their body then turn your body back to a side control, forcing the wrist onto the ground *(Figure 15.28–15.29)*.

6. Turn your body toward the right to take a position similar to a scarf hold. This will start to put pressure on their shoulder *(Figure 15.30)*.

7. Step your right foot over your partner's head, then continue to turn to the right until they tap. This prevents them from sitting up to take the pressure off their shoulder. Turn your body slowly for training safety *(Figure 15.31)*.

If applying this in a self-defense situation dangerous enough to justify causing serious damage to their shoulder, this lock can be applied in one sharp motion.

Americana / Keylock from Mount

The Americana or keylock is a joint lock that targets the shoulder using the arms as the primary leverage point, locking in the opposite direction of the Kimura. Follow the description below when applying this lock to your partner's right shoulder. Reverse all the directions if applying it to the left shoulder.

1. Once you've established mount, try to shift your weight so that it's resting on your partner's chest, rather than his hips. This makes it harder to shift your balance through bridging or shrimping *(Figure 15.32)*.

2. Push your partner's right arm toward the ground close to their shoulder placing your right elbow next to their ear. While doing this action, grip their arm with your right hand on the wrist and your left hand on the elbow, thumbs joined with your fingers (not gripping around) *(Figure 15.33–15.34)*.

3. For extra leverage, tuck your left elbow into your hip to allow you to put more of your weight into the push. If you need just a little more push to get the arm down, you can also use your forehead to drive more weight *(Figure 15.35–15.37)*.

4. Slip your left hand under your partner's tricep and grab your right wrist. This action may also be done more easily before the arm touches down on the ground if your partner is resisting *(Figure 15.38–15.39)*. As you do this action, hook your right leg around their left leg, bringing your foot

up while driving your hip down *(Figure 15.40–15.41)*. Your left knee should spread wider to increase your base. These leg positions help prevent from being bridged and rolled.

5. For training safety, slowly draw your partner's arm toward your hip, gradually raising their elbow with your own until they tap. If applying this in a self-defense situation dangerous enough to justify causing serious damage to their shoulder, this lock can be applied in one sharp motion.

Americana/Keylock from Side Control

Follow the description below when applying this lock to your partner's right shoulder. Reverse the directions if applying it to the left shoulder. The best time to try this lock is when your partner's arm is up, whether it's up by their head or tucked into a guard under your body. We'll demonstrate it from the latter position, as it is the more difficult of the two.

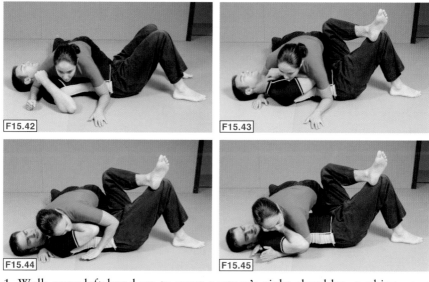

1. Walk your left hand up to your partner's right shoulder, pushing your bicep between their body and their arm *(Figure 15.42–15.45)*.

2. Straighten your left leg out, dropping your hips down to put more of your weight on your partner. Come up on your right foot, turning your upper body to create space around your partner's right arm *(Figure 15.46–15.47)*.

3. Grab your partner's right wrist with your right hand, thumb joined with your fingers *(Figure 15.48)*.

F15.48

F15.49

F15.50

4. Drop your right knee to the ground, while driving your partner's wrist to the ground, close to their shoulder. The knee action allows you to drop more of your body weight into the push *(Figure 15.49–15.50)*.

F15.51

F15.52

5. Slide your left hand under your partner's tricep and grab your right wrist, thumb joined together with your fingers *(Figure 15.51)*.

6. Roll your partner's wrist over with your right hand then slowly draw it toward their hip, gradually raising their elbow with your own until they tap *(Figure 15.52)*. If applying this in a self-defense situation dangerous enough to justify causing serious damage to their shoulder, this lock can be applied in one sharp motion.

Straight Ankle Lock

The straight ankle lock is a joint lock that targets the ankle using the arm as the primary leverage point. Follow the description below when applying this lock to your partner's right ankle. Reverse all the directions if applying the lock to the left ankle. Because the pain receptors are often not as sensitive in the ankle, use extreme caution when applying this lock in training.

F15.53   F15.54

1. The most common position for applying the straight ankle lock is from within an open guard. Start by forcing your partner's left leg to the ground with your right hand, caus- F15.55 ing their right leg to come up against your body *(Figure 15.53–15.54)*.

2. Draw your right knee over your partner's left leg then fall to your side, placing your left foot on their right hip *(Figure 15.55)*.

F15.56   F15.57

3. Lift and turn your hips toward the right to create space and shoot your left hand through the opening *(Figure 15.56–15.57)*.

F15.58   F15.59

4. Make a fist with your left hand and grab it with your right hand *(Figure 15.58)*.

5. Keeping your left foot on your partner's hip and your knees squeezed together, arch your hips and back slowly *(Figure 15.59)*. For training safety, applying pressure on the ankle until they tap. If applying this in a self-defense situation dangerous enough to justify causing serious damage to their ankle, this lock can be applied in one sharp motion.

Heel Hook

The heel hook is a joint lock that targets the knee using the arms and legs to twist the joint. This lock puts pressure on your partner's knee on the ACL. Because the pain receptors aren't as sensitive in this area, use extreme caution when applying this lock in training. If on the receiving end, for your own safety, tap if the position is secure rather than waiting for enough pressure for it to become painful as this may only happen when damage is caused.

Follow the description below when applying this lock to your partner's right knee. Reverse all the directions if applying the lock to the opposite side.

1. Like the straight ankle lock, the most common position for applying the heel hook is from within an open guard. Start by forcing your partner's left leg to the ground with your right hand, causing their right leg to come up against your body *(Figure 15.60)*.

F15.60   F15.61

2. Draw your knee over your partner's left leg then fall to your side, placing your left foot on their right hip *(Figure 15.61–15.62)*.

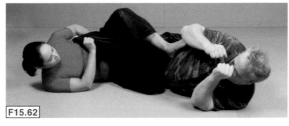

F15.62

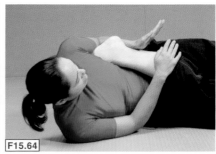

F15.63

F15.64

3. Hook the blade of your left arm around your partner's right heel, clasping your hands together *(Figure 15.63–15.65)*.

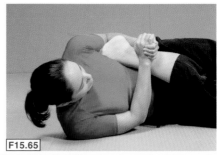

F15.65

F15.66

F15.67

4. Keeping your foot pressed into your partner's right hip, going very slowly for training purposes, turn your body toward the right, pressing the outside of the heel toward the ground using the blade of your left arm *(Figure 15.66–15.67)*. When doing this in training, the receiving partner should tap when pressure is achieved rather than waiting for pain in order to protect the joint.

When training, if your partner doesn't tap as a secure lock is achieved, don't follow the action through as you may inadvertently cause damage to their knee. If applying in a self-defense context, do so only in a situation dangerous enough to justify causing serious damage to your attacker's knee.

CHAPTER 16

Defending Against Joint Locks

In the last chapter, you learned some of the most common joint locks used by submission grapplers. Now that you have some understanding of how they work, you can learn the most important thing about them for street defense purposes; how to defend against them. Getting caught on the receiving end of a joint lock can be dangerous, having the potential to cause crippling injuries from which it can take years to recover, so it's well worth learning the defensive tactics in this chapter.

The Nature of the Attack

Like neck restraints, joint locks are commonly used in submission grappling but not as commonly on the street. But for the same reasons listed in Chapter 13 regarding the prominence of submission grappling sports, it is important to learn what is involved in these types of attacks to prevent them from being used against you.

In a submission grappling competition, the expectation is for opponents caught in these types of attacks to submit by tapping out so as to prevent injury. In a street context in which there are no rules however, there is less likely to be the same sense of sportsmanship, and the attacker may simply keep applying pressure until they cause injury to their victim. Even if an attacker doesn't intend to cause injury, if they are drunk or high, they may not be able to stop themselves before it's too late.

The joint locks most commonly used in a submission grappling context attack either the elbow or the shoulder. As a general rule, the best way to keep your hands and arms from being vulnerable to joint locks is to keep your arms bent and close to the body. Doing this allows you to make fuller use of your body to keep them protected. When your hands and arms are further from your body, it makes it easier for your attacker to use leverage against you to control your arm.

Similar principles apply to knee and ankle locks. If you're on your back and your guard is open, you should keep your legs and feet closer to your body. Of course, if your guard is open in a self-defense context, you should

F16.1   F16.2

be trying to kick at your attacker's vital targets, which makes it a lot more difficult for them to gain enough control over your legs to apply a leg lock. If you're not kicking your attacker for whatever reason, and you're maintaining an open guard, it is important to keep your feet on the front of your attacker's body and not hanging off their sides. Having your feet hanging off their sides makes it very easy for an experienced submission grappler to drop back into a leg joint lock.

Beyond these very early prevention points, there are a wide variety of methods for escaping each of the various commonly used joint locks. This book demonstrates methods that allow for quick escape, combining body shifting and attacks to vital targets, and can be used by people of different body types. But with the variety of methods that are out there, don't heistate to experiment with a number of different approaches to see which ones work best for you. If you're consulting submission grappling resources though, remember to make adjustments if you intend to use their techniques for the purposes of a self-defense situation since your goal is not to win a competition, but to escape.

*Tip: If all else fails, tap out. As with neck restraints, don't hesitate to use a submission grappler's training against them. They are trained to release their submission attacks when their "partner" taps out. The more experience they have, the more likely they are to do this, even if they aren't in a training context. While you shouldn't rely on this as a primary defense, if you're stuck and in danger of injuring a joint, it's definitely worth a try.

Body Shifting Principles to Keep in Mind

The body shifting principles used to defend against joint locks are specific to the lock against which you are defending. Some utilize shrimping, some bridging, and some use simple body weight transfer principles that are specific to the lock against which you're defending. Whatever form of body shifting you're using, there are two ways they can allow you to prevent the lock from being fully applied. They either A) allow you to move with the pressure to prevent the lock from tightening, often leading to a stronger defensive position, or B) allow you to block the pressure, making their efforts ineffective.

More details on this will be covered in the instructional portion on the defenses against each type of joint lock.

Vital Targets to Attack

It's important to note that attacks to vital targets are more useful earlier in the defensive process against joint locks, before they are being applied. If you're able to obstruct your attacker's joint lock early in their attempt, there are fewer risks involved in using attacks to their vital targets. If you're going for vital targets as a primary technique in a last ditch effort to get out of a lock, there is a strong risk that they'll be able to finish it before you're able to land an effective strike. That's why it's important to defend against the joint lock by using body shifting, blocking the lock, or a combination of the two *before* you attempt to use any vital targets to aid your escape. When it comes to specific vital targets, there are different options against different positions. These will be covered in the instructional portion on the defenses against each type of joint lock.

Defense: Arm Bar (Early)

The arm bar is the most commonly performed joint lock. It is most commonly performed from either the mount or the guard position. We will cover the defense from the mount position in this section, but whatever position you are defending from, the principles for defending against a standard arm bar are the same.

F16.3   F16.4

1. When an attacker with a submission grappling background grabs a wrist or otherwise controls one of your arms from the mount position, there is a good chance they will try to follow up with an arm bar *(Figure 16.1–16.4)*. Realizing this will help you react quicker when they do try it. We'll show two primary ways to establish this control. One way is to post their foot by your shoulder while latching onto the arm. Another way is to grab your wrist while they swing their leg over your head and across your body, as seen in the above left photo.

2. When they apply the arm bar, regardless of the method, roll with their momentum and come up to your knee, bending the elbow of the arm being attacked, tucking your hand to your head as though answering a phone. The goal is get your elbow below their leverage point between their legs.

3. Once your elbow is protected, drive your shoulder and/or chest into your attacker's leg to stack them on top of each other. This action will simultaneously free your wrist from their grip. Drive from your legs to get the most weight you can behind the action.

4. Strike one or more vital targets to help prevent the attacker from re-engaging their attack as you come to your feet.

Defense: Arm Bar (Late)

If you aren't able to stop the arm bar early in the attempt, there is still another chance to defend against it as they gain the application position.

F16.11

F16.12

1. As your attacker locks in their position to apply the arm bar, you must act quickly. Slip your opposite arm behind the forearm of the arm being locked, reaching across and grabbing onto your attacker's hip. This takes the pressure off your elbow joint and puts it harmlessly into your forearm.

*Note: Make sure it is between your elbow and wrist, not your elbow and shoulder. If you make this mistake, it will actually increase the pressure on your elbow *(Figure 16.12)*.

F16.13

F16.14

2. Once your arm is protected, roll up onto your knees (if you're not already on them) *(Figure 16.13–16.14)*.

3. Come to your feet, keeping one leg forward for stability. Turn your palm down *(Figure 16.15–16.16)*.

F16.15

F16.16

F16.17   F16.18

4. Pull your arm out of the grip sharply then stack your attacker's legs away from you. If the attacker is still a threat, strike the ribs or other vital target before stepping away from them *(Figure 16.17–16.18)*.

Defense: Kimura From the Guard

F16.19   F16.20

1. As your attacker moves into position to apply the kimura on your right arm, drive your upper body into your attacker all the way up into their right arm pit. As you do so, hook your right hand under your right thigh to block the lock *(Figure 16.19–16.21)*.

F16.21

2. Press your right knee into your attacker's wrist to gain leverage then pull your arm out of the lock *(Figure 16.22–16.23)*.

3. As soon as you're free, posture up and get to your feet, using any strikes necessary. See Chapter 12 for examples of ways to escape the guard position.

Defense: Kimura (From Side Control)

1. As your attacker attempts to apply a Kimura on your right side, shrimp onto your right side, tucking your elbow into your body. The elbow must be tightly pulled into your body otherwise your attacker may be able to switch his attack and go for an Americana *(Figure 16.24–16.25)*.

2. Immediately draw your right knee under your attacker's left arm. Use your knee to pry your arm out of the grip. This action can be facilitated by grabbing and squeezing your attacker's love handle *(Figure 16.26)*.

3. As soon as you're free, use one of the defenses shown in Chapter 11 to escape the side control position *(Figure 16.27)*.

Defense: Americana/Key Lock (From Mount)

F16.28   F16.29

1. To apply an Americana on your right arm, your attacker will start by controlling your wrist and forcing it to the ground with your hand up near your head *(Figure 16.28)*. As they do this, they let go of their left hand in order to slip it under your tricep to apply the lock. To prevent them from getting their left arm in position, act one step ahead of them and pin your right arm to the ground as quickly as possible. To get the Americana, your attacker will now have to dig his left hand under your arm and force it through. To make it harder for them, push into the ground with your left leg to transfer more of your body weight into the arm *(Figure 16.29)*.

2. As your attacker tries to force their way under, pin your attacker's left foot with your right foot then bridge your hips up and roll to your right side. You can facilitate this movement by striking their ribs with your knuckle and following through *(Figure 16.30)*.

F16.30

F16.31   F16.32   F16.33

If your attacker has their right leg hooked around your left leg, you'll need to work your leg free of the hook and tuck it in to your hips first in order to do the bridge *(Figure 16.31–16.33)*.

3. Roll up to your knees and use any strikes necessary to get to your feet *(Figure 16.34)*.

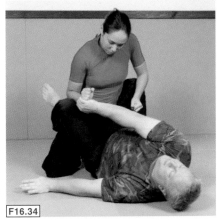

4. If your attacker posts their left arm to prevent from being rolled, you can grab it, draw it to your hip then re-attempt the bridge *(Figure 16.35)*.

If you aren't able to do this though, your attacker will likely attempt to re-establish their mount. In this case, you would simply draw your arms into your chest then try to escape the mount *(Figure 16.37)*. See Chapter 7 for defenses against a mounted attacker.

Defense: Americana/Key Lock (From Side Control)

1. As your attacker attempts to apply an Americana on your right side, shrimp onto your right side, tucking your elbow into your body *(Figure 16.38)*.

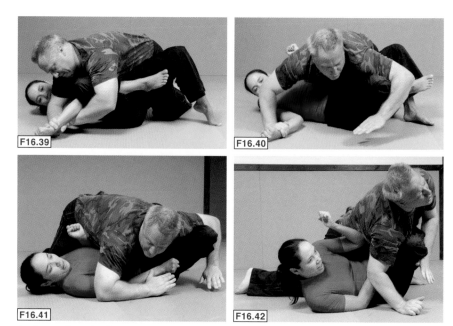

2. Immediately draw your right knee under your attacker's left arm. Use your knee to pry your arm out of the grip. This action can be facilitated by driving into your attacker's ribs with an elbow strike *(Figure 16.39–16.42)*.

3. As soon as you're free, use one of the defenses shown in Chapter 11 to escape the side control position.

Alternative Escape

If the above technique is difficult because your limbs are longer or you lack the flexibility in your hips, try the alternative escape below. These two techniques may also be used in combination with each other. If you get stuck on one, you can switch to the other or vice versa.

1. As your attacker attempts to apply an Americana on your right side, raise your right arm, pinning it to the ground to slow your attacker's attempt *(Figure 16.43)*.

2. Shift your feet away from your attacker *(Figure 16.44)*.

F16.45   F16.46

3. Bridge your hips up and roll toward your attacker while simultaneously thrusting your right arm up *(Figure 16.45–16.46)*.

F16.47   F16.48

4. Come to your knees, supporting your upper body on your left hand then pull your right arm free *(Figure 16.47)*.
5. Drive your knee into their ribs to help prevent the attacker from re-engaging their attack as you come to your feet *(Figure 16.48)*.

Defense: Straight Ankle Lock (Early)

F16.49   F16.50

1. To apply this lock on your left ankle, your attacker will wrap their right arm around it and then roll back, controlling your body with their legs. To escape this lock before they get it locked down, go with their momentum as they roll back, coming up to your feet. If they have a shirt on, grabbing onto it make it even easier to use their momentum *(Figure 16.49–16.50)*.

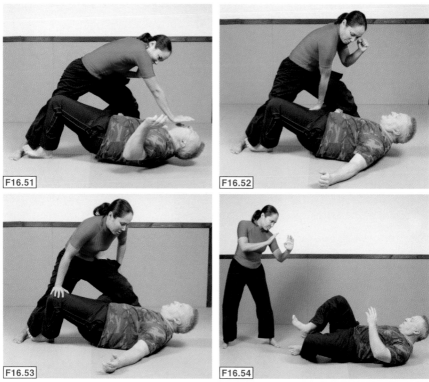

2. As soon as you're on your feet, attack any available vital targets in the head area to create an opportunity to pull your leg out and escape. Eyes, nose, skull and ears are all potential options. Groin may also be a target depending on their positioning *(Figure 16.51–16.54)*.

Defense: Straight Ankle Lock (Late)

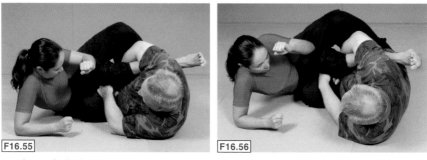

1. If you failed to stop the straight ankle lock early and your left leg is caught in the ankle lock, sit up and push your leg further into your attacker's arm grip. This forces them to put the pressure on the tibial nerve in your calf, which can still be painful, but more bearable than being locked in at the ankle *(Figure 16.55–16.56)*.

2. Push your left knee around your attacker's right leg and to the ground. This will get your foot on an angle, making it hard to apply pressure on your calf effectively.

3. Your attacker will likely do one of two things, both of which you can respond to. If they try to keep their hips open and force you back with their knee, their groin is exposed so you can easily strike it then pull your leg out of the lock *(Figure 16.57–16.58)*.

4. If your attacker closes their knees together to try and control your leg, post your left foot up by their shoulder then attack any available vital targets on the head to create an opportunity to pull your leg out and escape. Eyes, nose, skull and ears are all potential options *(Figure 16.59–16.62)*.

Defense: Heel Hook

This is an extremely dangerous knee lock. The reason why it is so dangerous is that there are very few pain receptors in the knee. While not painful in the initial stages of the lock, it quickly escalates into action that can cause serious damage to the knee because there is no pain to warn you of the danger. As soon as you get caught into this position, you must react immediately as they start to apply pressure for the best chance of escaping without injury to the knee.

1. To get into position to apply a heel hook to your left leg, your attacker will wrap their right arm around it and

then roll back, controlling your body with their legs the same way they would if they were applying a straight ankle lock. You can use the same early defense as we showed for straight ankle lock *(Figure 16.63–16.64)*.

F16.64

F16.65

F16.66

F16.67

F16.68

2. If your attacker has gotten you into the heel hook position, roll onto your knees toward your left, away from the pressure, bending them as you roll *(Figure 16.65–16.68)*.

F16.69

F16.70

3. From your hands and knees, kick back into your attacker's leg or buttocks and pull your leg out from your attacker's arms, getting to your feet as quickly as possible *(Figure 16.69–16.70)*.

Alternative Escape

F16.71

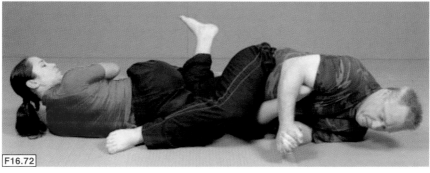

F16.72

1. If you roll quickly, you could also end up on your opposite side, rather than on your knees *(Figure 16.71–16.72)*.

F16.73

2. If this happens, push on your attacker's elbow with your right foot to pull your leg out from your attacker's arms, getting to your feet as quickly as possible *(Figure 16.73)*.

CHAPTER 17

Defending Against Knife Attacks on the Ground

In the last chapter, you learned to defend against joint locks on the ground, which have the potential to cause crippling injuries. It's great to be able to defend against these, but fortunately for us in a self-defense context, it takes skill and training for attackers to use these kinds of moves in the first place. This is training that the average person isn't as likely to have. Knives, on the other hand, serve as an equalizer. A person doesn't need to have any training at all to be dangerous with a knife. Even if you have experience with knife defense, the concepts are different when applied on the ground. That's why it's important to learn knife defense concepts that are specific to ground encounters.

What Makes Knives So Dangerous

Knives are particularly difficult to defend against as weapons for a variety of reasons. One of the main reasons is that anyone using a knife is more or less an expert, due to their long history of experience using them. As children, we learned to cut our food and intuitively know how much force it takes to slice or stab into a piece of meat. We have all used knives to prepare meals, and various professions require regular use of knives. In most societies, men of all ages carry pocket knives as tools. This makes it that much more important to understand that you can never underestimate someone armed with an edged weapon.

When it comes to dealing with knife attacks, distance is your friend. But if a knife is drawn in the middle of a ground encounter, you don't have this luxury, making knife attacks on the ground even more dangerous than when you are in a standing position. In general, knife attacks come fast and end fast. In most cases they come as a spontaneous attack, one that comes in extremely fast, making it that much more difficult for you to react effectively. The average edged-weapon fight lasts no more than five seconds. Within these few seconds, serious bodily injury or death is inflicted. As a result, a person's first reaction to the knife attack is critical for determining the outcome.

Critical Concepts for Surviving Knife Attacks

There are a few important concepts to remember no matter what techniques you use to defend against knives, whether they are the ones presented in this book, ones that you learn at your martial arts school, or ones you improvise yourself.

Assume There is a Knife When the Hand "Disappears"

If you're in the middle of an aggressive situation or an assault, be very aware of where your aggressor's hands are. If the hand suddenly reaches toward their waistband or into a pocket, expect it to come out with a knife. If you are standing and in a position where you can maneuver, you would create distance or put physical barriers between you and the attacker. On the ground, you probably won't have this luxury. That being said, there is a brief window of time in which the knife hand is caught up in the act of drawing the knife. If you react quickly (and you're close enough) you can stop it before it is fully drawn, which is much safer than dealing with it mid-swing. If a standing attacker draws a knife while you're prone on the ground, get to your feet as quickly as possible if you can safely do so. You are better able to maneuver and have a better chance of gaining control of the knife or escaping when on your feet. If you can't get to your feet before your attacker gets to you then you may have to deal with the knife from the disadvantageous position of being on the ground.

Yell "KNIFE!"

When a knife is drawn in an altercation, yell, "KNIFE!" as loudly and forcefully as you can. This increases the odds that someone might hear and witness what is going on and/or contact the local authorities to intervene. It may also serve to distract your attacker making them pause or hesitate in their attack. It also helps focus your energy on mounting a strong defense rather than freezing in fear at the lethal nature of the attack. It can also serve to alert other people who may be at risk, whether it's your friends or a partner if you're in law enforcement.

Get Control of the Weapon Arm

The safest way to deal with a knife after it's been drawn when you're unarmed, on the ground and don't have the option to create distance is to get control of the weapon arm. Once you have control, you should either strike out at the most effective vital targets available to you or displace your attacker's body through body shifting techniques to put yourself in a position where you can. The specific approach you take, of course, will be dependent on the type of defensive position you're in. We will cover a number of examples in the technical portion of this chapter.

Knives are Most Dangerous to the Inside of the Body

All the body's main arteries and organs are on the inside of the body (i.e. neck, eyes, head, torso, and the inside of your arms and legs) so you should try to keep these areas protected when dealing with knife attack, whether you're on the ground or on your feet. The arteries include: carotid, subclavian, brachial, radial, iliac and femoral. For a 188 lb, 5'10" man at a heart rate of 130 BPM (beats per minute), cuts to the above arteries can cause shock within 1 second to 1 minute and 55 seconds, unconsciousness in 17 seconds to 2 minutes and 52 seconds, and death in 23 seconds to 3 minutes and 50 seconds, depending on the affected artery. The organs at risk include the eyes, heart, stomach, liver, spleen, intestines, and genitals. While knife wounds to organs vary in severity, all are serious injuries. It is a good rule of thumb to always protect the inside of your body when defending against a knife.

Getting Cut is Not the End of the Fight

Many knife wounds don't incapacitate the victim. There are countless stories of knife attacks in which victims suffered numerous cuts and still survived. In *Prison's Bloody Iron*, the authors tell a story in which they watched two men involved in a knife fight in prison that were each cut over 40 times before the fight was broken up by the guards. In another case reported by the authors, a man was stabbed four times in the lungs (a fatal wound if left unattended). He ran down three flights of stairs after being stabbed before he collapsed about five minutes later. He was then rushed to the prison hospital where a fellow prisoner applied masking tape over the wounds, which kept the man alive long enough to get him to the city hospital for proper treatment. Needless to say, a person being attacked with a knife should keep fighting until they are no longer capable of fighting back. A winning attitude is vital.

Knives are Lethal Weapons

This point is obvious, but it has important implications on how people react to knives. Their brutality and lethality usually lead to heightened fear, which results in increased combat stress. Also, because knives are lethal weapon, in general, you're justified in using lethal force. As such, in most societies, you can use whatever means you have at your disposal provided it is a "real" attack and not your 8-year-old nephew having a hissy fit with a steak knife, for example. Police officers are taught to use their firearms if they can get enough distance to safely do so (approximately 21 feet). Unarmed defenders can usually legally justify using weapons of opportunity that constitute lethal force (including edged weapons, bludgeoning weapons, etc.) when fearing for their lives. These are general rules and not legal advice though, so it is a good idea for readers to familiarize themselves with the laws for their area with regards to self-protection.

*Note: If it needs to be stated, you are at such a severe disadvantage when dealing with a knife wielding attacker on the ground, even if you develop a high level of skill at defensive techniques such as the ones presented below. Only rely on physical defense to create opportunities for tactical disengagement and escape if there are no other options and your life is at stake.

Defense: Knife Attack from a Standing Attacker

The concept presented for this defense can be applied whether the attacker is slashing or stabbing. The only thing that would change is the angle from which the arm is controlled and the angle from which you kick at available vital targets.

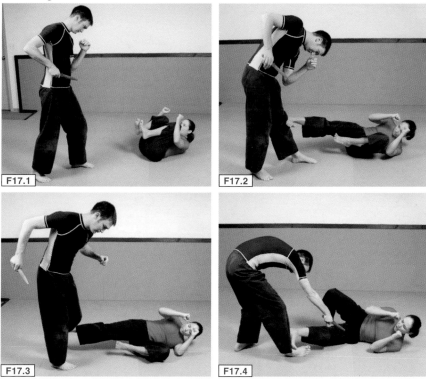

1. Keep your legs and arms bent in tight to your body so they act as a shield for the more vulnerable inside areas of your body *(Figure 17.1–17.3)*.
2. A standing attacker must get closer to you and bend down to your level in order to slash at you with a knife when you're on the ground. If they come in straight, aiming for the inner part of your body and/or legs, deliver a side kick (or multiple side kicks) to any available targets. In this context, side kicks are safer as it keeps the inner parts of the legs more shielded as you kick, whereas a turtle kick can leave the inside of your leg exposed making you vulnerable to cuts to the femoral artery *(Figure 17.4)*. If you're lucky, you could land a kick that will immobilize your attacker, or cause

them to fall over when done to a leg mid-step, but your kicks may only serve to distract them or cause them to hesitate. Either way, get to your feet as quickly as possible, when you have the opportunity to do so safely.

3. Alternatively, your attacker may try to move in around your legs to attack you with the knife. Block the arm at the wrist with your forearms and shins. As you block, immediately wrap your arms around the wrist, pinning it to your shins. Keep your arms and legs close to your body. The farther they are from your body, the less you'll be able to leverage your body weight for control *(Figure 17.5–17.7)*.

4. Once you have established control, use your legs to kick at any vital targets that are available to you. Usually the shins, knees or groin present the best opportunities, longer legged people may also be able to target the head *(Figure 17.8–17.9)*. Keep kicking until you can get up safely. If you have the opportunity to do so, take the knife. If you get ahold of the knife it may be better toss to it away at a safe distance than to wield it for defense depending on the situation. The reason for this is that if someone walks in on the scenario they may think that you are the aggressor.

Defense: When the Hand Disappears (Mount)

Ideally, you want to stuff your attacker's attempt to grab a hidden knife (or other weapon) before it's in hand, and failing that before it's in use. That being said, you may not react quickly enough to stop it in time. If the attacker starts to stab or slash at you, the following defense can still be used, but the risk of getting cut or getting cut more seriously is higher as you try to gain control over the knife wielding arm while it's in motion.

1. If your attacker is mounted on you and suddenly reaches toward their waistband, assume they are reaching for a knife.
2. Immediately grab the arm and hug it tight into your body, bridging your hips. This allows you to control the weapon arm while breaking your attacker's balance.

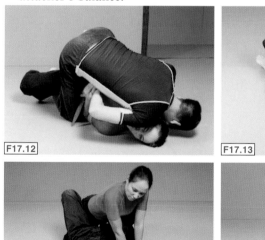

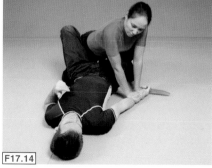

3. Using your foot, pin the foot on the same side of the arm you've controlled then bridge and roll toward it *(Figure 17.12–17.13)*.
4. Roll up to your knees and control the knife hand by pinning the wrist to the ground with both your hands, placing your weight on it *(Figure 17.14)*.

5. Maintaining your control of the knife hand, drop your close elbow into the groin, yelling "DROP THE KNIFE!" When the attacker is sufficiently weakened, take control of the knife. It may be better toss it away at a safe distance than to wield it for defense depending on the situation for reasons previously stated *(Figure 17.15)*.

Defense: When the Hand Disappears (Attacker Between the Legs)

As with the previous defense, you ideally want to stuff your attacker's attempt to draw a hidden knife (or other weapon) before it's in hand, and failing that before it's in use. If you're unable to do so in this context, you have two options. One is to try and gain control the knife mid-swing, similar to the last defense presented. But, because your legs are free, you also have the option to kick out at your attacker to create an opportunity to get back to your feet. Getting control of the knife is the safest option if you can do so quickly, but if you can't for whatever reason, kicking your way out is better than nothing.

F17.16 F17.17 F17.18

1. If your attacker is kneeling between your legs and suddenly reaches toward their waist band, assume they are reaching for a knife *(Figure 17.16)*.
2. Immediately grab the arm and hug it tight into your body. As you take control of the knife and break your attacker's balance, throw your leg over their back to control their body *(Figure 17.17–17.18)*.

F17.19 F17.20

3. Use your legs to kick any accessible vital targets. Different ones will be available depending on the length of your legs relative to your attacker. If you have shorter legs you should be able to drive your heels into your attacker's kidneys or the back of the head *(Figure 17.19–17.20)*.

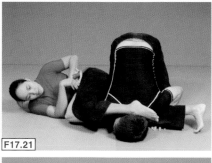

4. If you have longer legs, you may find it easier to drive your heel into the ribs or deliver a roundhouse-style kick to the back of their head. Once you have sufficiently weakened your attacker, swing your leg over your attacker's head, keeping the knife arm between your legs. If they have let go of the knife, take control of it, and keep or dispose of it appropriately for your situation *(Figure 17.21–17.24)*.

5. If your attacker is still holding the knife, yell "DROP THE KNIFE!" while smashing their wrist into the ground. If they still don't let go, peel their fingers back and break them until they do. Take control of the knife and get to your feet as soon as quickly as possible. Keep or dispose of the knife appropriately for your situation *(Figure 17.25)*.

Defense: Knife at Your Throat in Mount

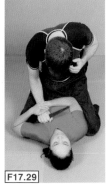

F17.26   F17.27   F17.28   F17.29

1. If an aggressor is holding a knife at your throat, you must get control of the knife hand in a way that poses the least risk of being cut in the neck area. In Figure 27.26, if the defender were to draw the knife hand to their left, there would be a greater risk of getting cut, so they would draw it to her right shoulder instead. If the defender were to draw the knife to their left *(Figure 17.28)* there would be a greater risk of getting cut, so they would draw it to their left shoulder instead.

F17.30   F17.31   F17.32   F17.33

2. Pin your attacker's leg with your own foot on the side on which the knife is being held *(Figure 17.30)*.
3. Bridge your hips up and roll in the direction your attacker's leg and wrist are pinned *(Figure 17.31)*.
4. Roll up to your knees and get control of the knife hand by pinning the wrist to the ground with your hands, leaning your weight on it *(Figure 17.32)*.
5. Maintaining your control of the knife hand, drop your close elbow into the groin, yelling "DROP THE KNIFE!" When the attacker is sufficiently weakened, take control of the knife. Keep or dispose of the knife appropriately for your situation *(Figure 17.33)*.

Defense: Knife at Your Throat From Between Legs

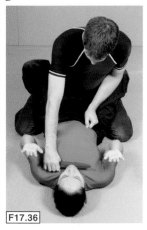

1. As with the last defense, control of the knife hand in a way that poses the least risk of being cut in the neck area *(Figure 17.34–17.37)*.

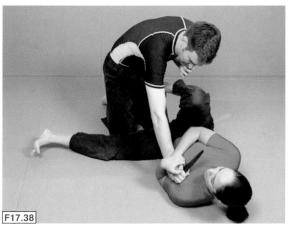

2. Once you've established control of the knife hand, shrimp onto your side in the direction of the knife-wielding hand *(Figure 17.38)*. Kick at vital targets you can reach. The head, ribs and solar plexus are a few potential options.

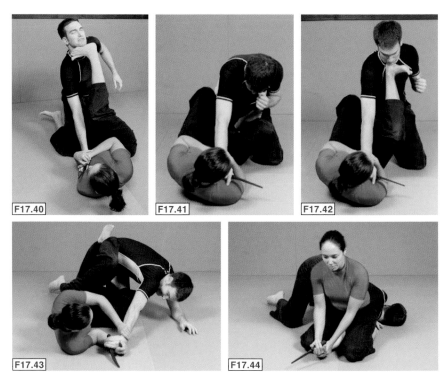

3. Push your attacker's wrist of the knife-wielding arm to the floor, pinning it with both hands and your closest knee. If you're controlling it from the back of the arm, you can simply apply pressure to the elbow, while yelling "DROP THE KNIFE!" *(Figure 17.40–17.44)*

   If you're controlling it from the inside of the arm, use your inside arm to deliver elbow strikes to your attacker's head while yelling "DROP THE KNIFE!" *(Figure 17.45)*

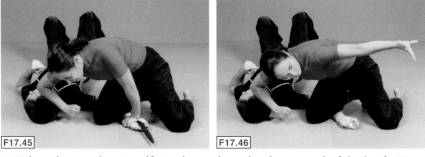

4. When the attacker is sufficiently weakened, take control of the knife. Keep or dispose of the knife appropriately for your situation *(Figure 17.46)*.

CHAPTER 18

Defending Against Multiple Attackers on the Ground

In the last chapter, you learned a few approaches to defending yourself should you find yourself in the dangerous situation of facing a knife on the ground. Facing a knife presents a high degree of risk to your safety, whether it's on the ground or in any other type of defensive scenario. A situation that can be equally dangerous is one in which you have to defend against more than one attacker, and on the ground this presents an even greater threat.

The Dangers of Defending Against Multiple Attackers

Facing more than one attacker has a number of inherent dangers. Naturally, one of the biggest risks is to be overwhelmed to the point that you aren't able to mount an effective defense. This is in large part physical, of course, but the psychological impact can make things worse. A person is more likely to experience higher levels of combat stress due to the potentially lethal nature of a multiple attacker situation. Combat stress causes an adrenaline dump, which can result in several physical/mental effects that put you at a particular disadvantage when dealing with multiple attackers. These include funnelled concentration, tunnel vision and auditory exclusion (also known as 'tunnel hearing'). These are conditions that affect how you perceive your surroundings.

Funnelled Concentration

This is a mental condition that affects the way we perceive the world around us. When under combat stress, our mind often funnels our concentration on what we perceive as our main threat, resulting in intensified sound, tunnel vision, and heightened visual clarity. The mind directs the sense organs to get as much information on our threat as quickly as possible. While this can be a gift when dealing with a single threat, we pay a price. Things we aren't focused on can literally disappear from our awareness.

Tunnel Vision

These are conditions that affect how you perceive your surroundings. When you experience tunnel vision and tunnel hearing, your mind focuses on what it perceives as the main threat.

Tunnel vision results in a zoom lens effect representing an approximate loss of 20% of your peripheral vision on either side. In addition, the eyes begin to move in a "saccadic" fashion, a rapid, jerky, irregular scanning motion, which allows them to pick up more visual clues at a time when the conscious interaction between the brain and the eye might be too slow. The brain doesn't process all that the eye reports during this movement, only what the eye stops on. This means that the vision is stuttered and you only see things in glimpses.

Auditory Exclusion

In high stress conditions, the brain usually chooses one of the five senses to provide the most relevant information at that moment. In most cases, the vision is chosen as the primary sense. This results in the brain excluding information from the other senses as it processes the situation. The condition is often described as a high-pitch ringing in your ears. Extraneous sounds seem to recede into background noise. This is partially due to the adrenalin in your system, which causes the blood vessels to dilate in and around the ears, making it harder to hear. Cognitive dissonance, on the other hand, prevents the mind from prioritizing those sounds. This means that you may not be able to receive and/or process important audio information that comes from threats outside your primary focus.

Reducing the Impact of Combat Stress

The above three conditions can make it easier for multiple attackers to triangulate you or otherwise coordinate their attack, making it harder for you to mount an effective defense. There are, however, ways to reduce the impact of their effects, whether you're dealing with multiple attackers, a knife attack or any other lethal treat.

Preparing for Combat Stress

Being prepared, both physically and mentally, to deal with combat stress, helps you to cope better when you experience it for real. Training in physical defense techniques helps of course, but more specifically, training to deal with multiple attacker scenarios, helps you develop a general approach ahead of time so that you're more likely to cope competently despite the effects of combat stress, or in some cases, as a result of it. Many law enforcement organizations advocate mental rehearsal as a practice to reduce the body and mind's reactions to combat stress. Mental rehearsal is also helpful because in training we aren't able to fully replicate what may occur in a real situation due to safety reasons or practicality. Imagine yourself going through the scenario, making it as true to life as possible. One of the most important aspects of this form of training is to always visualize yourself winning, training yourself to never give up, whether you get hurt, stabbed, shot, etc. You want to anticipate stressful situations so you can be better prepared for them.

Regulating the Effects Combat Stress

Scanning your field of vision is an important technique for coping with tunnel vision. While under combat stress, you should practice looking side to side, up and down to increase your field of vision. This serves to provide more visual cues or threats that may be overlooked while experiencing tunnel vision. It's a good idea to do this any time you're under the effects of combat stress, whether you are dealing with multiple attackers or only one. You're more likely to get caught off guard when you're pre-occupied with a single person, and there's always the possibility that others could step in.

While under stress, we have a tendency to shorten our breaths, thereby reducing our oxygen intake and increasing the effects of adrenalin. Consciously taking smooth, elongated breaths can help counter the tendency to rely on shallow breathing, which often occurs while under stress, thereby helping to control the body's reaction.

Principles for Defending Against Multiple Attackers

Beyond the management of combat stress, there are a number of principles that can help you to mount a more effective defense against multiple attackers. You are at a severe disadvantage when dealing with multiple attackers. Only rely on physical defense if there are no other options and your life is at stake. In cases when you have no choice, use physical defense techniques that follows these strategies:

Get Off the Ground. If you have the opportunity or can create the opportunity to do so, get back on your feet. When standing you're more maneuverable and can more easily prevent attackers from triangulating than you can when on the ground. Whatever physical techniques you use, getting back on your feet should generally be the goal in multiple attacker scenarios.

Make Your First Strike Count. Your first strike will be an important determining factor in the outcome of the situation. If you are aggressive and land a strong, effective kick on your first attacker as they enter, it may cause the other attackers to hesitate or stop their approach, giving you an opportunity to get to your feet before they get to you. Yelling strong aggressive commands loudly like, "No!" "Stop!" or "Back off!" as you strike can also help increase the intimidation factor while potentially gathering witnesses who might either intervene or call for help.

Keep Moving. Use the body shifting drills introduced in Chapter 3, keep your head as far from your attackers as possible while putting your legs in a position that allows you to more easily deliver strong kicks to your attackers' legs. You'll likely have to change directions quickly, swinging your legs one direction or another, more so than using the stepping movements. This may seem like an impossible task with more than one attacker coming at you, and you may get hit in the process. The key is to try and make your attackers' blows land on less damaging targets while making your own blows effective at stopping or slowing their advance.

Protect Your Head. One way multiple attackers are likely to attempt to overwhelm you is to surround you and kick you while you're down. A kick to the head can easily knock you unconscious and has the potential to cause brain damage or even kill you. Keep your head out of reach of kicks as much as possible. Failing this, shield your head with your arms strongly to absorb the force of the kicks as much as possible while you find opportunities to strike back.

Be Aggressive and Unpredictable. Aggressiveness and unusual actions can cause your attackers to hesitate. One of the most effective concepts for ground defense we teach in our women's self-defense classes is going "alley cat crazy." Since the participants don't have the benefit of ongoing training to learn all the various components that make for effective ground defense, they need a concept that can put to use with little to no training. The idea is that if someone is getting on top of you, you scream aggressively, kick your legs and strike out with your arms in a frenzy of movement, like an alley cat gone crazy. This action alone can shock a potential attacker and see the person as a dangerous and therefore an unappealing victim. As for unpredictability, there are a wide variety of ways you can add this to your defense. You could use different types of rolls to put space between you and your defenders. You could arc your legs in an unexpected way causing your attackers to flinch back. It's impossible to tell you all the different ways to be unpredictable. It's mostly about seizing opportunities as present themselves in the situation you are in. Anything can work once when it's done in a way that comes as a surprise.

Use Weapons of Opportunity. Objects in your surroundings can be used as weapons to help improve your defensive capabilities when in the disadvantaged situation of a multiple person attack. This could come in the form of throwing a rock at a person's head to cause them to flinch, disrupting their attack. Or this could mean throwing a stool in one of their path's causing them to trip. Or perhaps you might be able to use a back pack to shield against kicks or roll under a table, making it harder for them to predict your defense. Use any tools in your surroundings if they will help improve your defense. See Chapter 4 for more information on weapons of opportunity.

Don't Let Them Get on Top of You. The more your attackers "pile" onto you, the less you can move, the more energy you have to use and the harder it is to get back to your feet. If one attacker gets on top of you, react immediately and aggressively to keep others from pressing the advantage. If more than one person gets on top of you, particularly when you have one person controlling your upper body while the other one controls your legs, your opportunities for defense are severely compromised so you should be prepared to do whatever it takes to avoid this.

Defensive Drill: Multiple Standing Attackers from the Ground

It's difficult to simulate this situation in a way that is both realistic and safe for training purposes, considering that the defender is likely to be targeting the legs with their kicks. Even when restraint is exercised, there is always the chance you could accidentally injure someone's knee. The drill below is one way to train for this situation using body shields.

F18.1

F18.2

The defender starts on the ground with two or more attackers surrounding them holding body shields *(Figure 18.1)*.

The attackers' goal is to swarm the defender, forcing the defender to the ground using the body shields to keep them from getting to their feet *(Figure 18.2)*.

F18.3

F18.4

F18.5

The defender's goal is to get back to their feet and get away. To do this they must kick their attacker's body shields to simulate kicking their legs, to create the opportunity to their feet. Kicking higher than the legs gives attackers more of a chance to grab them, so in general, going for leg targets is safest *(Figure 18.3–18.5)*.

*Note: Attackers should hold the body shields away from their legs because a kick to the shield can penetrate through to the knee if they're not careful.

F18.6

F18.7

The defender may need to use additional strikes if attackers close in as they get to their feet. This may come in the form of a kick, punch, elbow strike, or anything else that makes sense.

Once on their feet, the defender should try put their attackers between each other, using strikes if necessary, then escape at the first opportunity *(Figure 18.9–18.12)*.

F18.8

F18.9

F18.10

F18.11

F18.12

Defensive Applications: Multiple Standing Attackers from the Ground

For illustrative purposes, below is one example of how a 2-on-1 situation could play out ideally using these defensive concepts. Of course you can't count on things necessarily going this well and you have to be ready to adapt to less than ideal circumstances. That being said, if you do end up in this disadvantaged situation, you should visualize yourself "winning" the encounter, rather than focusing on the difficulties and setbacks.

As the closest attacker moves in, the defender delivers a strong side kick to their knee, causing a painful injury to the knee, which makes them stumble backward and away*(Figure 18.13–18.14)*.

This causes the second attacker to hesitate, but they still come in to kick, which the defender blocks with their arms, which are being used to shield their head *(Figure 18.15–18.17)*.

The defender answers back aggressively delivering an elbow strike to the attacker's groin, a palm strike to the chin; using the momentum of her strikes to help her get to her feet and escape *(Figure 18.18–18.19)*.

F18.18   F18.19

*Remember: There is no one "correct" way to get back to one's feet in training or in reality. Every situation is different. The important thing is to discover what movements and strikes tend to work best for you, but to be open to unorthodox tactics that may go outside your usual strategies based on the opportunities you face.

Bibliography

— Dorsey, Greg, John Sommers, and Steve Uhrig. *"Future of Non-lethal Force Training-Reality Based & Integrating Techniques for Non-Lethal Force Training."* ASLET Use-of-Force Training Seminar, originally presented at the Los Angeles Airport Hilton and Towers, Los Angeles, California, July 10-12, 1997.

— Drzwiecki, Steve. *Survival Stress in Law Enforcement. Traverse City: 2002.*

— *Dunston, Mark S. "Instructor's Corner: Ground Fighting -- Assaults on Police Officers," Calibre Press Street Survival Newsline #630. April 2003.*

— *Grosz , Christopher and Michael D. Janich. Contemporary Knife Targeting. Boulder: Paladin Press, 2006.*

— *Jenks, Harold J and Michael H. Brown. Prison's Bloody Iron. El Dorado: Desert Publications, 1978.*

— *Lewinsky, Bill. "Stress Reactions Related to Lethal Force Encounters," The Police Marksman, May/June 2002.*

— *Siddle, B. Pressure Point and Control Tact. Millstadt: Pressure Point Control Tactics Management Systems Inc, 1998), 2-3. Quoted in Steve Drzwiecki, Survival Stress in Law Enforcement. Traverse City: 2002.*

— *Sylvain, Georges J. Can-Ryu Jiu-jitsu 2000. Ottawa: Georges J. Sylvain, 2003.*

— *The Phenomenon of Auditory Exclusion <http://www.atlanticsignal.com/mh3/pages/tpoae.html>, Atlantic Signal LLC, 2005 (Accessed 26 Sept. 2011).*

— *Wagner, Jim. Reality-Based Personal Protection. USA: Black Belt Communications LLC, 2005.*